RAW MEMES

Illustrated Quotes from
Robert Anton Wilson

RAW MEMES

Illustrated Quotes from
Robert Anton Wilson

composed by
Richard Rasa

HILARITAS PRESS

RAW Memes

Copyright © 2022 Richard Rasa

Print: ISBN: 978-1-952746-14-7
eBook: ISBN: 978-1-952746-15-4

First Edition: 2022, Hilaritas Press
eBook Version 1.0: 2022, Hilaritas Press

Cover Design by Rasa
Interior Design by Pelorian Digital

Quotes used with the joyful permission of the Robert Anton Wilson Trust

Photos of RAW by Bastian Staeuber Jermutus, Daisy Eris Campbell, Dan Dion, David Jay Brown, Duncan Harvey, James Nye, Jonathan Greet, Lance Bauscher, Marlis Jermutus, Richard Rasa, Roger Ressmeyer, Tom Sperlich, and unknown others.

Some backgrounds contributed by Brummbaer & amoeba
Nuit drawing, Wikimedia, A. Parrot

Hilaritas Press, LLC.
P.O. Box 1153
Grand Junction, Colorado 81502
www.hilaritaspress.com

Contents

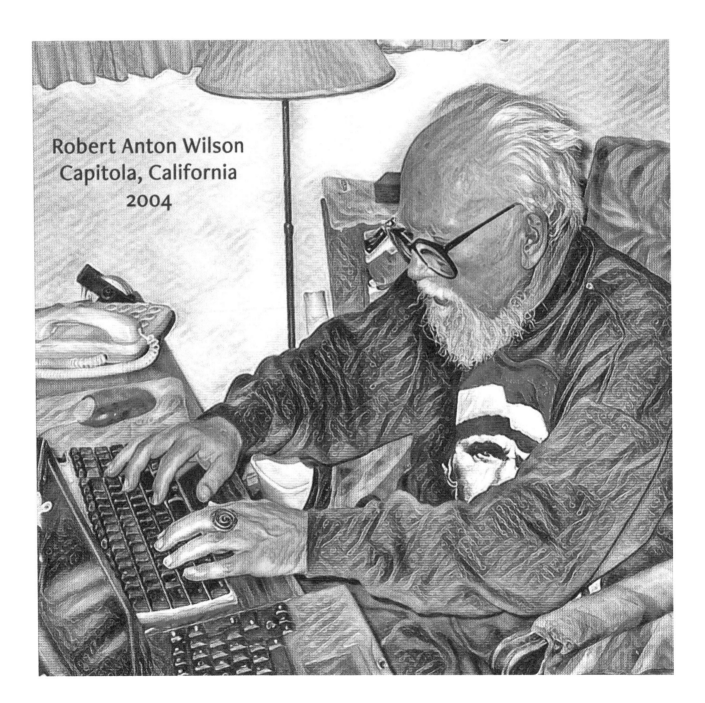

Robert Anton Wilson
Capitola, California
2004

Introduction

In an email to Robert Anton Wilson's GroupMind email list, Bob hesitantly announced his candidacy to run for governor in the 2003 California special election. He was hesitant because of his age and poor physical health, but he was convinced by his friends in the GroupMind to run as a digital candidate, and simply make pronouncements from the comfort of his connection to Internet.

Bob loved to converse with his friends via email, and he got emails from his friends every day. He picked out certain ones to comment on and sent those to the whole GroupMind. Threads of discussions in follow-up emails often ensued, and there was a lot of inspired and often thoughtful jocularity.

After Bob entered the political ring, a lot of his emails started to define the policies that concerned him, and they were often framed as the Position Papers of his new satirical Guns and Dope Party. Many of the ideas, he claimed, were inspired by a wise ostrich named Olga. He was pretty liberal about what he included in the platform. Position Paper #23 was actually a joke that my mother had sent to me in an email, and I had forwarded on to Bob. To be honest, I've always had the suspicion that sending Bob my mother's joke was the straw that broke his resistance to entering politics. It was that, and I suspect the prospect of doing it all on the computer screen without straining his aching post-polio syndrome legs.

But he didn't easily agree to be a candidate. GroupMind members, in email after email, tried to talk him into running, and with every entreaty, Bob said no, repeatedly and emphatically. In one email he wrote,

> I will not run and if elected will not serve. In the years
> left to me I wanna do SERIOUS work, not
> muck about in political bullshit
>
>   --bob

In another email he pushed back again,

> NO,NO, A THOUSAND TIMES NO!!!!!!! The
> synergetic trajectories of Universe cannot move in an
> omnibenevolent vector, but only in an omnilethal
> one, from within the political paradigm.
> EVERY MAN AND EVERY WOMAN IS A TSAR
>   --bob

At one point someone suggested Paul Krassner (who was following the discussion as a member of the GroupMind) would make a great Lieutenant Governor if Bob won the election. Paul also declined. He wrote,

> Thanks anyway, but hermits don't make good
> politicians. - pk

One GroupMind member, Kai, had what many of us thought was a great point. He wrote,

> It is the political strategy of Mark Emery of the BC
> Pot Party to ALWAYS run for everything he can. Not
> because he thinks he has a chance but because it lets
> him make speeches for the public record.

The other major candidates Bob was running against were Arnold Schwarzenegger (who eventually won, or at least they swore the guy in) and Arianna Huffington. With Arnold's Austrian accent, Arianna's Greek accent, and Bob's rather heavy at times Brooklyn accent, I made a joke about no one understanding the debates.

Still, noting his concern about what he called the War on Some Drugs, Bob protested,

> I'm old, I'm sick, I'm overworked-- find another
> Leader. Besides, Huff has the same policy as me on
> the issue that matters the most to me, medical
> freedom (no Tsarism) --bob

Then my mother sent me this joke:

> Little Tony was sitting on a park bench munching on
> one candy bar after another. After the 6th candy bar,
> a man on the bench across from him said, "Son, you
> know eating all that candy isn't good for you.
> It will give you acne, rot your teeth, and make you fat.
>
> Little Tony replied, "My grandfather lived to be 107 years old."
>
> The man asked, "Did your grandfather eat 6 candy bars at a time?"
>
> Little Tony answered, "No, he minded his own fucking business."

As I say, maybe Little Tony tipped the scales. After I sent the joke to Bob, the next email we got from him was this:

> After refusing many pleas to run for governor, I have
> reconsidered and now enter the race as an unofficial
> write-in candidate. After all, why shd I remain the
> ONLY nut in California who ain't running?

At that point if Bob was not "off and running," he was *off and writing*. With every new email to the GroupMind, he gradually fleshed out a description of his platform. Early on he wrote,

> If I announce [as I've considered] that God supports
> the Guns and Dope Party, how many of you will
> consider that 1. schizo to delusional 2. genuine
> Divine intervention 3. a con game 4. a hoax, satire, jape etc
>
> How do you rank the similar claims of Monkey-Boy (RAW's
> nickname for George Bush), Jerry Falwell, Son of Sam, the
> Tsars of Russia the Tsars of USA, Osama bin Laden the popes
> of Rome etc?
>
> anyway God has personally endorsed the GUNS
> AND DOPE PARTY and cursed Tsardom. He told me
> so, speaking through an ostrich named Olga who co-starred
> with Orson Welles in a thriller called SOUTHERN STAR.
> Those other guys are just jealous because the Voices don't
> speak to them and they have to fake it!

At this point Bob had been sending out party slogans and more and more anecdotes about his conversations with Olga. With all that glorious input, I opened Photoshop and created what were the first Guns and Dope Party graphics. Olga the ostrich and her fellow struthian politicians became the actors in my memes about the party. Bob published a dozen of those illustrations in his last book, *Email to the Universe.*

I'll tolerate your hobbies
if you'll tolerate mine.
Guns and Dope Party

Lance Bauscher, producer of the 2003 documentary, *Maybe Logic: The Lives and Ideas of Robert Anton Wilson*, offered to host a Guns and Dope Party website. I supplied the graphics, and some years later took over management of the site. I kept making various illustrations, many focused on Olga and her friends.

When Hilaritas Press was launched, I was rereading Bob's books, and making note of my favorite quotes. To advertise our new editions, I started using those quotes in memes. At the time of writing this, Hilaritas Press has published 20 books. I've created a couple hundred memes for Hilaritas Press, the RAW Trust and Flying Lasagna Enterprises. The memes in this collection of RAW Memes are my favorites.

Robert Anton Wilson wrote about so many different subjects and referenced the ideas of so many different notable people, that when I set out to figure out what order to use in presenting more than a hundred memes, I scratched my head for a long while before seeing some useable patterns.

I welcome you to speculate on the patterns I saw emerging, but honestly, I think this is a book that's fun to use in bibliomancy – and you don't even need to ask a question – just open the book to a random page and enjoy the trip.

Of course, it's also fun to read from beginning to end and enjoy the hidden narratives. Just remember…

Keep the Lasagna Flying!

Rasa
Weed, California
August 23rd, 2022

~•~

Our Hilaritas Press proof readers noted some "errors" in RAW's email comments used in this introduction. We suspect that some of those errors may have been the result of his post-polio syndrome, but because RAW loved to experiment with writing, heavily influenced by James Joyce, maybe they were intentional. All of these comments were transcribed exactly the way he wrote them in the emails, so we decided to leave them as is.

RAW MEMES

Reality is what you can get away with!

~•~

When I moved on to Brooklyn Technical High School, I encountered many bright, likable kids who were not Catholics and not at all right-wing in any respect. They naturally angered me at first. (That is the function of Correct Answer Machines: to make you have an adrenaline rush, instead of a new thought, when confronted with different opinions.) But these bright, non-Catholic kids — Protestants, Jews, agnostics, even atheists fascinated me in some ways. The result was that I started reading all the authors the nuns had warned me against — especially Darwin, Tom Paine, Ingersoll, Mencken and Nietzsche.

I found myself floating in a void of incertitude, a sensation that was unfamiliar and therefore uncomfortable. I retreated back to robotism by electing to install a new Correct Answer Machine in my brain. This happened to be a Trotskyist Correct Answer Machine, provided by the International Socialist Youth Party. I picked this Machine, I think, because, the alternative Correct Answer Machines then available were less "Papist" (authoritarian) and therefore less comfortable to my adolescent mind, still bent out of shape by the good nuns.

– Email to the Universe:

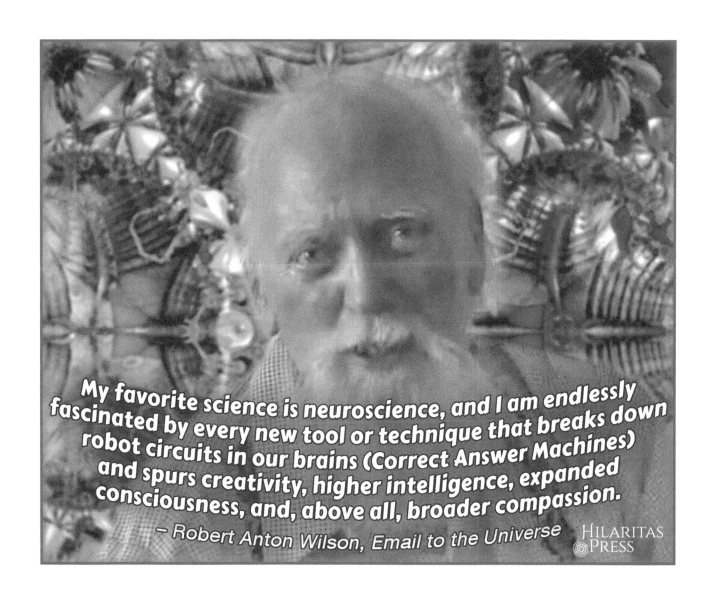

My favorite science is neuroscience, and I am endlessly fascinated by every new tool or technique that breaks down robot circuits in our brains (Correct Answer Machines) and spurs creativity, higher intelligence, expanded consciousness, and, above all, broader compassion.

– Robert Anton Wilson, *Email to the Universe*

HILARITAS PRESS

It was quite clear to me that faith could be as dangerous as the absence of faith. If your faith wasn't strong enough, God would let the devil torture you after you died; if your faith was too strong, He'd let the devil torture you right now, as a test. It was a "Choose this way and lose, or chose the other way and lose" situation — what Gregory Bateson later labeled a "double bind."

I gradually realized that the only way out of this was to be born non-Catholic, and I had missed that option. Once you were born Catholic, there was no way out, because you could not question anything the nuns told you. Questioning was "the sin of Pride" and absolutely guaranteed the most extreme forms of charbroiling and roasting and toasting and poaching and French Frying.

Most religions,
in this part of the world
teach us
"one correct answer,"
which we should accept
with blind faith;
worse,
they attempt to terrorize
us with threats of
post-mortem roasting,
toasting, boiling, broiling,
charbroiling and
freedomfrying if we ever
dare to think
at all, at all.

— Robert Anton Wilson,
Email to the Universe

HILARITAS
PRESS

My attitude is identical to that of Dr. Gribbin and the majority of physicists today, and is known in physics as "the Copenhagen Interpretation," because it was formulated in Copenhagen by Dr. Niels Bohr and his co-workers c. 1926-28. The Copenhagen Interpretation is sometimes called "model agnosticism" and holds that any grid we use to organize our experience of the world is a model of the world and should not be confused with the world itself. Alfred Korzybski, the semanticist, tried to popularize this outside physics with the slogan, "The map is not the territory." Alan Watts, a talented exegete of Oriental philosophy, restated it more vividly as "The menu is not the meal."

Belief in the traditional sense, or certitude, or dogma, amounts to the grandiose delusion, "My current model" — or grid, or map, or reality-tunnel — "contains the whole universe and will never need to be revised." In terms of the history of science and knowledge in general, this appears absurd and arrogant to me, and I am perpetually astonished that so many people still manage to live with such a medieval attitude.

– Cosmic Trigger I: Final Secret of the Illuminati

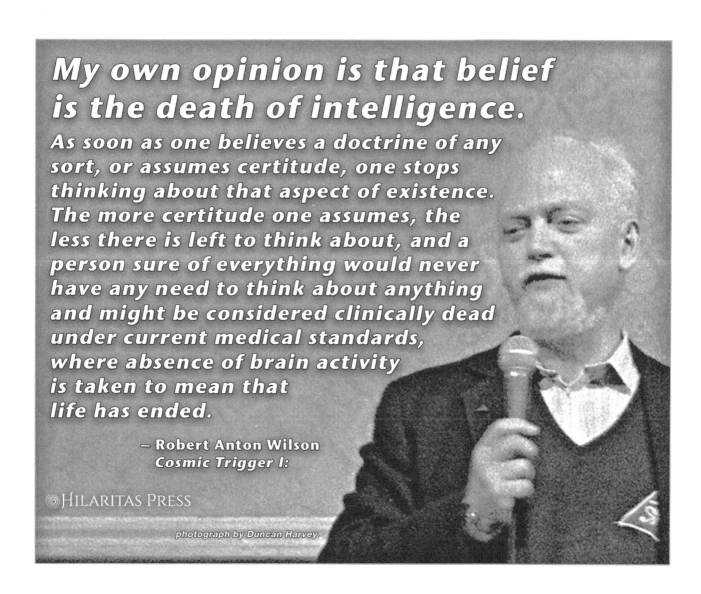

My own opinion is that belief is the death of intelligence. As soon as one believes a doctrine of any sort, or assumes certitude, one stops thinking about that aspect of existence. The more certitude one assumes, the less there is left to think about, and a person sure of everything would never have any need to think about anything and might be considered clinically dead under current medical standards, where absence of brain activity is taken to mean that life has ended.

— Robert Anton Wilson
Cosmic Trigger I:

HILARITAS PRESS

photograph by Duncan Harvey

15

Cosmic Trigger deals with a process of deliberately induced brain change through which I put myself in the years 1962-1976. This process is called "initiation" or "vision quest" in many traditional societies and can loosely be considered some dangerous variety of self-psychotherapy in modern terminology. I do not recommend it for everybody, and I think I obtained more good results than bad ones chiefly because I had been through two varieties of ordinary psychotherapy before I started my own adventures and because I had a good background in scientific philosophy and was not inclined to "believe" any astounding Revelations too literally.

Briefly, the main thing I learned in my experiments is that "reality" is always plural and mutable.

"I do not believe anything."

– Robert Anton Wilson, *Cosmic Trigger*

A phrase that has led to a swarm of misinterpretations.
Perhaps this quote from Quantum Psychology may help...

The "loss of certainty" does not mean
a descent into the void of solipsism.
It merely means a graduation
from the kindergarten level of
"yes" (100%)
or "no" (0%)
to the adult world of
"how closely can we
calculate the odds
on this happening?"
(5%? 25%? 75%? 95%?)
– *Quantum Psychology*

– *Cosmic Trigger I: Final Secret of the Illuminati*

Since the brain does not receive raw data, but edits data as it receives it, we need to understand the software the brain uses. The case for using E-Prime rests on the simple proposition that "isness" sets the brain into a medieval Aristotelian framework and makes it impossible to understand modern problems and opportunities. A classic case of GIGO, in short. Removing "isness" and writing/thinking only and always in operational/existential language, sets us, conversely, in a modern universe where we can successfully deal with modern issues.

Quantum Psychology: How Brain Software

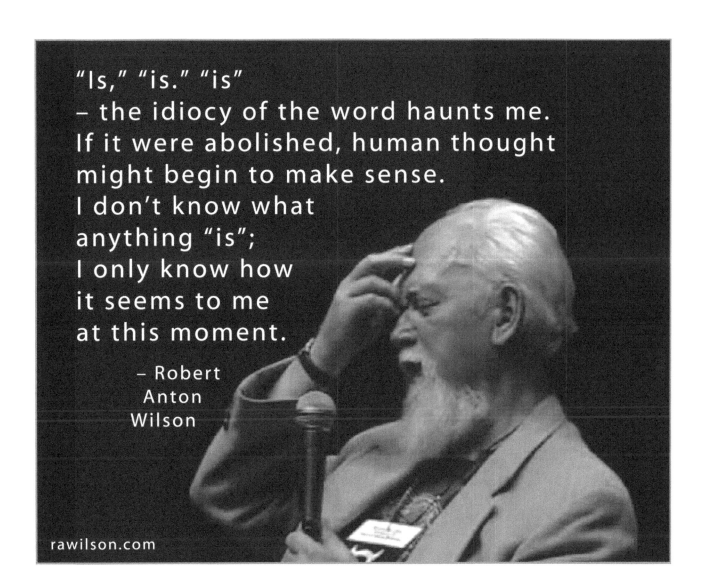

"Is," "is." "is"
– the idiocy of the word haunts me.
If it were abolished, human thought
might begin to make sense.
I don't know what
anything "is";
I only know how
it seems to me
at this moment.

    – Robert
      Anton
      Wilson

rawilson.com

Paul changed his major to biology and set out to find out precisely why every complex organism must die and what he could do about it . . . Paul is also an executive of the Bay Area Cryonics Society . . . In the mid-sixties Paul attended a lecture by Dr. Leary which he found to be a turning point in his own intellectual development. What Leary had communicated, Paul says, was that "everything we experience is hallucination, maya. The reality is a structural-mathematical-logical principle that we don't see. That is, each person creates his own universe out of his own neurological processes. Science is nothing else but the search for the unseen structural integrities that underlie these appearances."

Paul generalized this Buddhist-scientific synthesis into the theory that *we are information.*

"The ultimate reason that Immortality is possible," Paul told me, "is that *we are not the stuff we're made of.* Literally. You can trace a chemical through the body with radioactive tracers, but the body goes on after the chemical has left. We are not the chemicals but the pattern, the mathematical construct. You might say that the formula for Immortality is Cybernetics + DNA. But DNA is itself Cybernetics, the first application of cybernetic information theory to biology. DNA is entirely an information system, a programming system. Cybernetics is the key, the realization that *we are programmed and can be re-programmed.*"

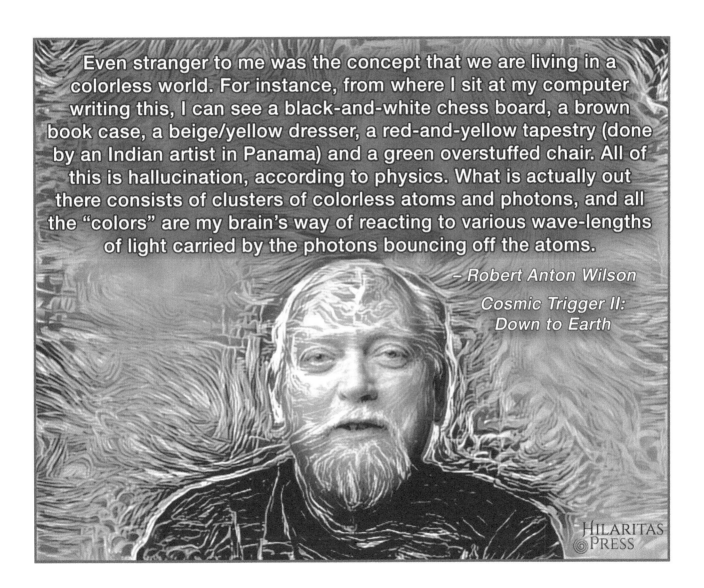

Even stranger to me was the concept that we are living in a colorless world. For instance, from where I sit at my computer writing this, I can see a black-and-white chess board, a brown book case, a beige/yellow dresser, a red-and-yellow tapestry (done by an Indian artist in Panama) and a green overstuffed chair. All of this is hallucination, according to physics. What is actually out there consists of clusters of colorless atoms and photons, and all the "colors" are my brain's way of reacting to various wave-lengths of light carried by the photons bouncing off the atoms.

– Robert Anton Wilson

*Cosmic Trigger II:
Down to Earth*

HILARITAS
©PRESS

– Cosmic Trigger I: Final Secret of the Illuminati

When Ahab told Starbuck, "All material things are but masks," he had in mind ancient Gnostic teachings, but he also anticipated most of the discoveries of recent neuro-psychology and brain science. "Material things" no longer appear solid ("material") to physics, and they no longer appear as *things* to the student of perception. They appear as abstractions, co-creations (combining external signals with our internal file-system), or as models, or maps, or metaphors (depending on which field of communication science we take our jargon from) — or as masks, in the language I have borrowed from Ahab.

We have manufactured all "material things" out of an ever-changing deluge of photons and electrons in an abysmal void. As Nietzsche first declared, "We are all greater artists than we realize." (Or, as the Zen *roshi* Hui Neng said, "From the beginning, there has never been a 'thing.'")

In the strip-tease, the dancer removes one article of clothing after another and then appears naked. This "tease," some think, derives from the myth of Ishtar, who descended to Hell and had to remove one article of clothing at each of its seven gates. At the last gate, naked, Ishtar entered Eternity. This symbolizes the removal of one mask after another until no masks remain. That state, as described by all who've lived it, transcends all words and categories: we cannot communicate the unmasked by any new mask.

We create our Masks, as God allegedly made the world, out of nothing. In both cases, the nothingness sometimes shows through.

– Robert Anton Wilson
The Wilderness Diary of Sigismundo Celine
The Historical Illuminatus Chronicles, Vol. 3, Nature's God

rawilson.com

– Cosmic Trigger III: My Life After Death

The seventh, metaprogramming circuit is the most recent in evolutionary time and seems to be located in the *frontal lobes*. That is why the traditional Hindu exercize to activate it is to fix the consciousness in the front of the forehead and hold it there, hour after hour, day after day, year after year, until the metaprogrammer awakes and you begin to perceive-create infinite realities where before there was only one static jail-cell "reality" in which you were trapped.

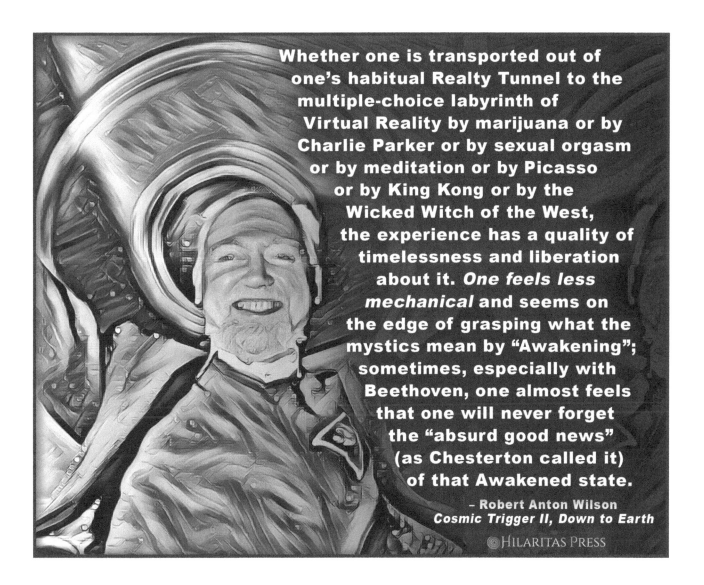

Whether one is transported out of one's habitual Realty Tunnel to the multiple-choice labyrinth of Virtual Reality by marijuana or by Charlie Parker or by sexual orgasm or by meditation or by Picasso or by King Kong or by the Wicked Witch of the West, the experience has a quality of timelessness and liberation about it. *One feels less mechanical* and seems on the edge of grasping what the mystics mean by "Awakening"; sometimes, especially with Beethoven, one almost feels that one will never forget the "absurd good news" (as Chesterton called it) of that Awakened state.

– Robert Anton Wilson
Cosmic Trigger II, Down to Earth

– Prometheus Rising

Considering the wide variety of philosophies available to any of us — nudism and Buddhism, scientific materialism and snake worship, Communism and vegetarianism, subjective Idealism and Existentialism, Methodism and Shinto, etc. — the fact that most people remain in the same reality-tunnel as their parents, does indicate that acculturalization is a mind control process. We are all giants, raised by pygmies, who have learned to walk with a perpetual mental crouch. Unleashing our full stature — our total brain power — is what this book is all about.

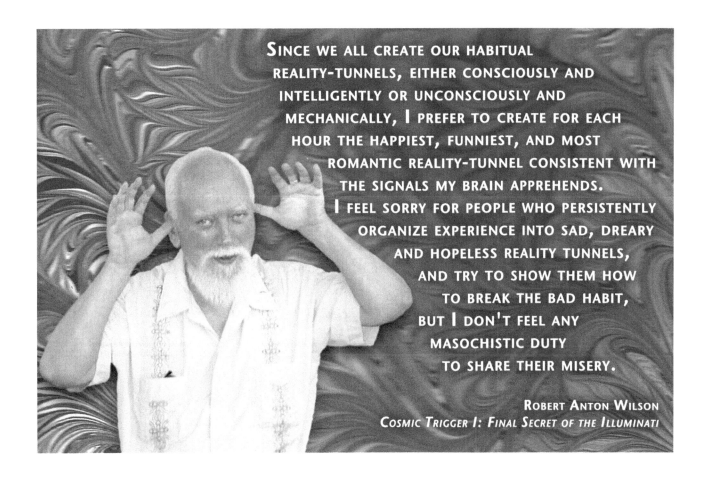

SINCE WE ALL CREATE OUR HABITUAL REALITY-TUNNELS, EITHER CONSCIOUSLY AND INTELLIGENTLY OR UNCONSCIOUSLY AND MECHANICALLY, I PREFER TO CREATE FOR EACH HOUR THE HAPPIEST, FUNNIEST, AND MOST ROMANTIC REALITY-TUNNEL CONSISTENT WITH THE SIGNALS MY BRAIN APPREHENDS. I FEEL SORRY FOR PEOPLE WHO PERSISTENTLY ORGANIZE EXPERIENCE INTO SAD, DREARY AND HOPELESS REALITY TUNNELS, AND TRY TO SHOW THEM HOW TO BREAK THE BAD HABIT, BUT I DON'T FEEL ANY MASOCHISTIC DUTY TO SHARE THEIR MISERY.

ROBERT ANTON WILSON
COSMIC TRIGGER I: FINAL SECRET OF THE ILLUMINATI

– *Prometheus Rising*

Blake said, "One Law for the Lion and Ox is tyranny." But even more, one "truth" for the Lion and Ox is impossible. There will always be different lanes for different brains, different scenes for different genes, different strokes for different folks.

We can negotiate meaningfully when we understand these neurological facts. When we think we have the "one true model," we cannot negotiate but only quarrel, and, in politics, usually we fight and kill.

– *Natural Law, Or Don't Put A Rubber On Your Willy*

There will always be different lanes for different brains, different scenes for different genes, different strokes for different folks.

– Natural Law, Or Don't Put A Rubber On Your Willy And Other Writings From A Natural Outlaw

HILARITAS PRESS

Whether the basis be genetic or sociological, there is no doubt that Irish Time is more relative than even Einsteinian time and seems infinitely flexible in all directions. For instance, if you hire a plumber and he tells you he will come "Tuesday week," that literally means one week from Tuesday but actually he'll come when he feels like it. "Tuesday fortnight," however, is even more daunting: it literally means two weeks from Tuesday but actually it indicates that the job sounds hard and the plumber will probably never come at all. Most events in Irish Time occur in the occult interval between temporarily uncertain Tuesday week" and for-ever uncertain "Tuesday fortnight," which I think is the time it takes Schrödinger's cat to jump from one *eigenstate* to another.

If you suspect that the wobbly time-sense of Eire can be explained entirely as a manifestation of the calculated procrastination of colonial peoples, you are probably missing the complexity of the Gaelic mindset. One story tells of the two clocks in Padraic Pearse Station, Dublin, which, of course, being Irish clocks always disagree. An Englishman, this story claims, once commented loudly and angrily on how "typically Irish" it was to have two clocks in a train station that gave different times. "Ah, sure," a Dublin man replied, "if they agreed, one of them would be superfluous."

Excerpt from The Land Where Bulls Are Pregnant By Robert Anton Wilson
Magical Blend, Issue 20, Aug-Sept-Oct 1988

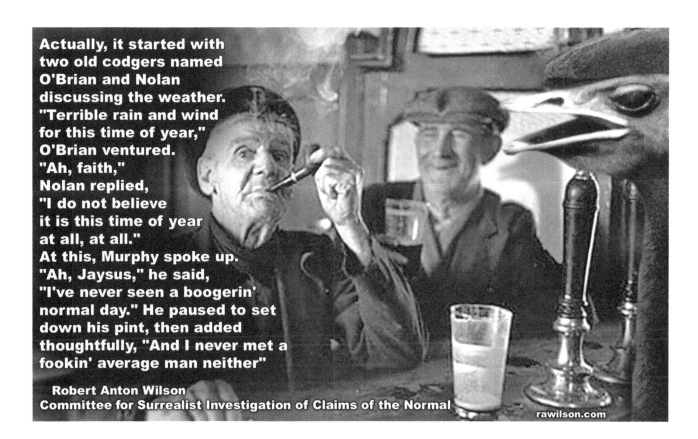

Actually, it started with two old codgers named O'Brian and Nolan discussing the weather. "Terrible rain and wind for this time of year," O'Brian ventured. "Ah, faith," Nolan replied, "I do not believe it is this time of year at all, at all." At this, Murphy spoke up. "Ah, Jaysus," he said, "I've never seen a boogerin' normal day." He paused to set down his pint, then added thoughtfully, "And I never met a fookin' average man neither"

Robert Anton Wilson
Committee for Surrealist Investigation of Claims of the Normal

rawilson.com

I once read an intelligent Fundamentalist tract. (There are intelligent Fundamentalists, just as there are honest politicians. Every miracle happens at least once!) The author argued that Satanists and black magicians are responsible for spreading the ideas that all humans can learn to develop occult talents, that we can achieve physical immortality and migrate off this planet, and that there is no limit to the expansion of human intelligence. Since I believe all those things, and have devoted much energy to propagandizing for them, I am very definitely a Satanist and a black magician, by this gentleman's standards.

– Natural Law, Or Don't Put A Rubber On Your Willy
And Other Writings From A Natural Outlaw

One of the first Discordian catmas (Other religions have dogmas, which are absolute beliefs. Discordianism has catmas, which are relative meta-beliefs.) was Kerry Thornley's Law of Fives, which holds that all incidents and events are directly connected to the number five, or to some multiple of five, or to some number related to five in one way or another, *given enough ingenuity on the part of the interpreter*. Usually, we would state this to novices without the crucial (italicized) final clause; it was up to them to discover the metaprogrammer and figure that part out for themselves.

– Cosmic Trigger I: Final Secret of the Illuminati

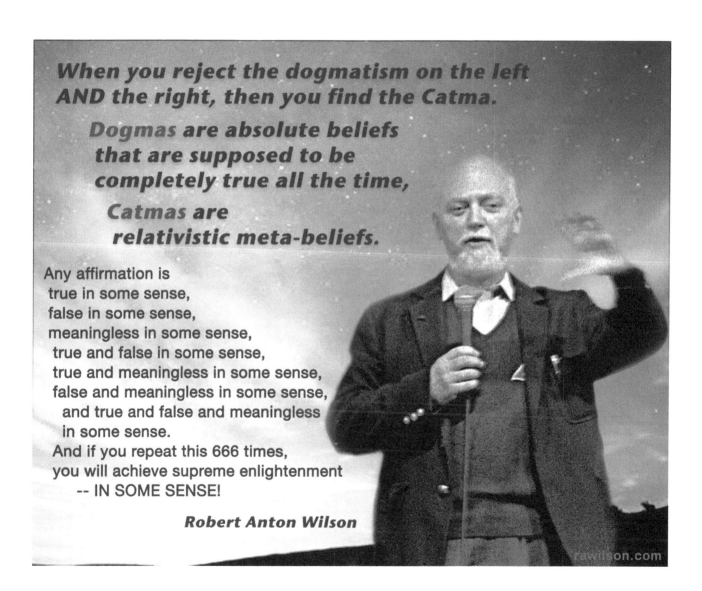

When you reject the dogmatism on the left AND the right, then you find the Catma.

Dogmas are absolute beliefs that are supposed to be completely true all the time,

Catmas are relativistic meta-beliefs.

Any affirmation is
true in some sense,
false in some sense,
meaningless in some sense,
true and false in some sense,
true and meaningless in some sense,
false and meaningless in some sense,
and true and false and meaningless in some sense.
And if you repeat this 666 times,
you will achieve supreme enlightenment
-- IN SOME SENSE!

Robert Anton Wilson

rawilson.com

Sad as it is to say, you never understand anything by merely reading a book about it. That's why every science course includes laboratory experiments, and why every consciousness-liberation movement demands practice of yogas, meditations, confrontation techniques, etc. in which the ideas are tested in the laboratory of your own nervous system.

The reader will absolutely *not* understand this book unless he or she does the exercizes given at the end of each chapter.

To explore the Thinker and the Prover, try the following:

1. Visualize a quarter vividly, and imagine vividly that you are going to find the quarter on the street. Then, look for the quarter every time you take a walk, meanwhile continuing to visualize it. See how long it takes you to find the quarter . . .

– Prometheus Rising

Whatever system dominates at a given time appears as the ego or self at that time, in two senses:

1. People who meet Mr. A when he has the Oral Submissive self predominant, will remember him as "that sort of person." People who meet him when he has the Semantic/rational self predominant remember him as another sort of person. Etc.

2. Due to state-specific information, as discussed earlier, when you have one of these selves predominant, you "forget" the other selves to a surprising extent and act as if the brain only had access to the information banks of the presently predominant self. E.g., when frightened into infantile Oral states, you may actually think "I am always a weakling," quite forgetting the times when your Anal Dominator self was in charge, or the Semantic or Sexual imprints were governing the brain, etc.

Quantum Psychology: How Brain Software
Programs You and Your World

Leary distinguishes eight types of intelligence. The first four are:

Bio-Survival Intelligence: seems mostly genetic and tells an animal or human how to find the nourishing and "supportive" and how to avoid the predatory or toxic.

Emotional-Territorial Intelligence: tells an animal how to read the body-language of another animal and know what the other animal is feeling (and, hence, what it will probably do next.)

Semantic Intelligence: is based on genetic potential and early imprints but mostly is learned slowly, over years, from peers and instructors. It allows us to understand one or two symbol systems (or even several if we are clever) and perhaps to create a symbol-system of our own, sometimes.

Socio-Sexual Intelligence: allows us to manage our social and sexual relations in ways that keep us reasonably happy or at least out of jail.

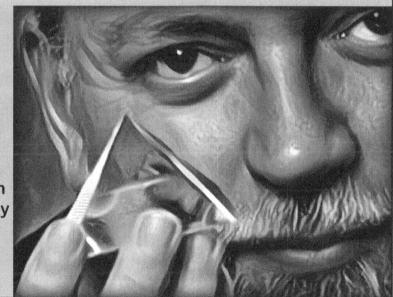

Robert Anton Wilson,
Cosmic Trigger II: Down to Earth

HILARITAS PRESS

I would consider it the height of intellectual laziness and mental incompetence to invoke the word "God" to cover the limitations of my imagination and vocabulary. Instead, I will conclude with the wise words of Aleister Crowley. When asked to define the Tao he said,

The result of subtracting the universe from itself.

Quantum Psychology: How Brain Software
Programs You and Your World

~•~

Editor's note: RAW switched the placement of Circuits 6 & 7 in some of his writings, and both RAW and Timothy Leary, when asked about that, said that it was an evolving model, and they had different thoughts at different times. For a detailed look at this issue, see the Afterword in *Prometheus Rising.*

~•~

Leary's other four types of intelligence, which are rare in our society, are:

Neurosomatic Intelligence: the "wisdom of the body" holistic physicians talk about;

Neurogenetic Intelligence: access to the "collective unconscious" or "species mind" where archetypes like the inward-turning spiral or King Kong are stored and, when activated, trigger leaps of intuition;

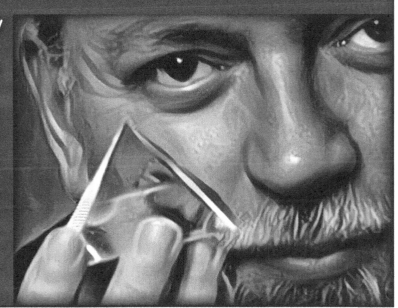

Metaprogramming Intelligence: the capacity to turn on and tune in to each type of intelligence as needed; and

Non-Local Intelligence: which enables one to endure "mystical" experiences without coming out of them as a raving loony.

Robert Anton Wilson,
Cosmic Trigger II: Down to Earth

HILARITAS PRESS

. . . the analysis of Perls, Hefferline and Goodman (in *Gestalt Therapy*) . . . explains that most people function on a level of "chronic low-grade emergency"; but Dr. Leary gives an evolutionary neurogenetic interpretation of why we misuse our nervous systems that way. Too much emotion by the parents or parent surrogates, when imprinting the second circuit, leads to chronic, daily, hour-by-hour emotionalism (consistent Circuit Two behavior) in the offspring, for the rest of their lives. This starts when the child stands up, and the later dexterity-analysis or engineering-logic facilities of Circuit Three are not imprinted until the child begins asking questions constantly and manipulating tools. Thus, in most people, reason remains — as all cynics have noted — the slave of emotion, and is generally used only to justify the reflexes (passions, compulsions) of the glandular system. Circuit Two checkmates Circuit Three.

When Circuit Five, rapture, is imprinted, the emotional circuits finally become relatively dormant; and then objective reason becomes possible, as Gurdjieff predicted. Circuit Five plus Circuit Three can checkmate Circuit Two.

– The Starseed Signals

Circuit Five plus Circuit Three can checkmate Circuit Two

— Robert Anton Wilson, The Starseed Signals

The 8 Basic Winner and Loser scripts

Circuit	The Eight Basic Loser Scripts	The Eight Basic Winner Scripts
1. Biosurvival	"I don't know how to defend myself."	"I will live forever, or die trying."
2. Emotional-territorial	"They all intimidate me."	"I am free; you are free; we can have our separate trips or we can have the same trip."
3. Semantic	"I can't solve my problems."	"I am learning more about everything, including how to learn more."
4. Sociosexual	"Everything I like is illegal, immoral, or fattening."	"Love and do what thou wilt "
5. Neurosomatic	"I can't help the way I feel."	"How I feel depends on my neurological know how."
6. Metaprogramming	"Why do I have such lousy luck?"	"I make my own coincidences, synchronicities, luck, and Destiny."
7. Neurogenetic	"Evolution is blind and "impersonal."	"Future evolution depends on my decisions now."
8. Neuroatomic	"I'm not psychic, and I doubt that anyone is."	"In the province of the mind, what is believed true is true, or becomes true within limits to be learned by experience and experiment." (Dr. John Lilly)

– *The Illuminati Papers*

Eight Circuits, eight circuits –
don't blow a fuse
Robotic behaviour –
is scripted to lose
Come be a winner,
a meta-programmer
Don't panic, don't panic
You're a karma mechanic

Tit! Bark! Maps! Sex!
Turn on, Get Cosmic!

Daisy Eris
Campbell's
Cosmic Trigger
the Play

Q: What is it about writing that you find so personally rewarding?

A: Well, I think it's a sexy kind of controlled schizophrenia. It's also kind of yoga, especially novel-writing. Full-time fiction writing is a constant daily exercise in getting outside one's own head and thinking and feeling the way other people think and feel. I often think of story-telling in terms of Gurdjieff's work. Gurdjieff, the Russian mystic, devoted most of his energy to teaching his pupils how to get outside their own egos and see the world the way other people see it. I've become very interested in his work in the last four or five years, and it has occurred to me that what he is teaching is what every good novelist learns if he sticks with being a writer. One can't create characters who are simply variations of oneself; that gets boring after a while. One must go way out and create characters who are nothing like oneself. When one does that, one really learns something about humanity. In that sense, I think novel-writing is more educational for the novelist than for the reader, especially when the most "evil" villains I can imagine start making clever remarks and developing ideas of their own and really "come alive."

– Email to the Universe: and other
alterations of consciousness

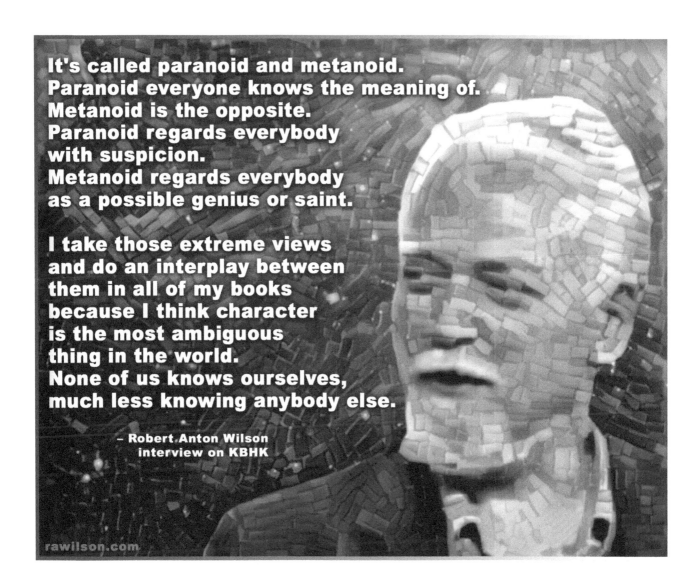

It's called paranoid and metanoid.
Paranoid everyone knows the meaning of.
Metanoid is the opposite.
Paranoid regards everybody
with suspicion.
Metanoid regards everybody
as a possible genius or saint.

I take those extreme views
and do an interplay between
them in all of my books
because I think character
is the most ambiguous
thing in the world.
None of us knows ourselves,
much less knowing anybody else.

— Robert Anton Wilson
interview on KBHK

rawilson.com

47

CD: Was black writer Ishmael Reed's *Mumbo Jumbo* the inspiration for *Illuminatus!*? Could you give us your reaction to *Mumbo Jumbo*?

Wilson: I didn't read *Mumbo Jumbo* until about 3 years after *Illuminatus!* was finished. The same is true of Pynchon's *Gravity's Rainbow*. The astonishing resemblances between those three books are coincidence, or synchronicity, or Higher Intelligence (take your pick). I love everything Ishmael Reed writes, and I once sent him an official Discordian certificate making him a Pope in the Legion of Dynamic Discord. One of the many hidden jokes in *Illuminatus!* (which is only the tip of the iceberg, being part of a much larger artwork called Operation Mindfuck) is that the Legion of Dynamic Discord actually exists, despite its preposterous sound, whereas some of the more plausible parts of the trilogy are deadpan put-ons. As e. e. cummings said to Ezra Pound, "You damned sadist, you're trying to force your readers to think!"

– The Illuminati Papers

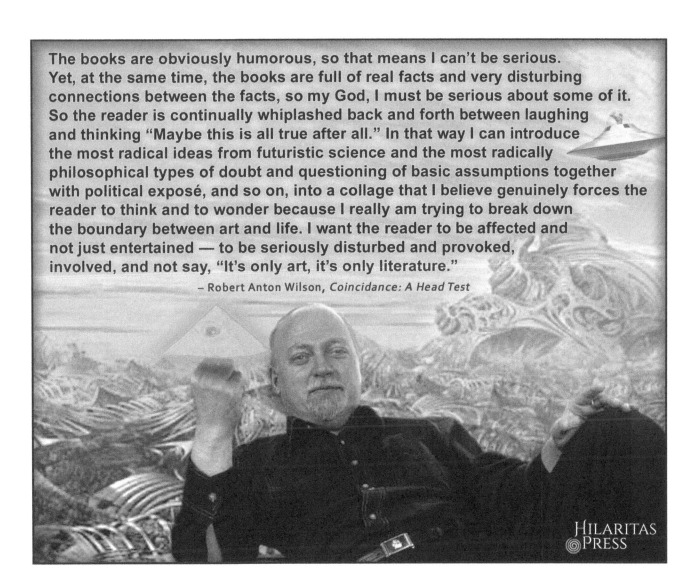

The books are obviously humorous, so that means I can't be serious. Yet, at the same time, the books are full of real facts and very disturbing connections between the facts, so my God, I must be serious about some of it. So the reader is continually whiplashed back and forth between laughing and thinking "Maybe this is all true after all." In that way I can introduce the most radical ideas from futuristic science and the most radically philosophical types of doubt and questioning of basic assumptions together with political exposé, and so on, into a collage that I believe genuinely forces the reader to think and to wonder because I really am trying to break down the boundary between art and life. I want the reader to be affected and not just entertained — to be seriously disturbed and provoked, involved, and not say, "It's only art, it's only literature."

– Robert Anton Wilson, *Coincidance: A Head Test*

HILARITAS PRESS

Many studies indicate that the neuropeptide activity in the brain – reassociating, or re-glossing, or moving from a rigid reality-tunnel to a multi-choice reality labyrinth – seems as important in healing as the chemical boost that neuropeptides give to the immune system. In other words, as our ability to process more and more information increases, our resistance to unwellness (in general) also increases.

A world of many options never "feels" as dreadful as a deterministic or mechanical world.

Quantum Psychology: How Brain Software
Programs You and Your World

"The joy of art is trying to convey what you perceive so that other people will perceive it more or less the same way. Art is a form of seduction...there are rapists in the intellectual world, they become politicians, the seducers become artists. We try to seduce people into our reality tunnels (rather) than leading them there with a gun. We are trying to get them into our reality. Our reality tunnel or our reality labyrinth. Which ever it is. In my case it's a reality labyrinth."

— Robert Anton Wilson
From Maybe Logic

rawilson.com

Politics, as I now see it, consists of normal human and mammalian demands disguised and artificially rationalized by pseudo-philosophy (Ideology). The disguise and rationalization *always* seems insincere when the other guys do it, but, due to self-hypnosis, becomes hallucinatorily "real" when one's own gang does it. I think at this stage of history, the disguise has become obsolete and counterproductive. *Make your demands explicit* (and leave out Natural Law and all Ideal Platonic Horseshit), and then you and the other guy can negotiate meaningfully. As long as both sides are talking metaphysics, each is convinced the other are hypocrites or "damned eejits."

– Natural Law, Or Don't Put A Rubber On Your Willy
And Other Writings From A Natural Outlaw

Every politician knows how to induce hypnosis, and very damned few people on the whole planet know how to de-hypnotize themselves. The world is not governed by facts or logic. It is governed by BS (belief systems).

Robert Anton Wilson
Cosmic Trigger II, Down to Earth

HILARITAS PRESS

Finnegan's paper began with the electrifying sentence, "The average Canadian has one testicle, just like Adolf Hitler — or, more precisely, the average male Canadian has 0.96 testicles, an even sadder plight than Hitler's, if the average Anything actually existed." He then went on to demonstrate that the normal or average human lives in substandard housing in Asia, has 0.51 vaginas, cannot read or write, suffers from malnutrition and never heard of Silken Thomas Fitzgerald or Brian Boru. "The normal," he concluded "consists of a null set which nobody and nothing really fits." Thus began the science of 'patapsychology . . .

– Email to the Universe
and other alterations of consciousness

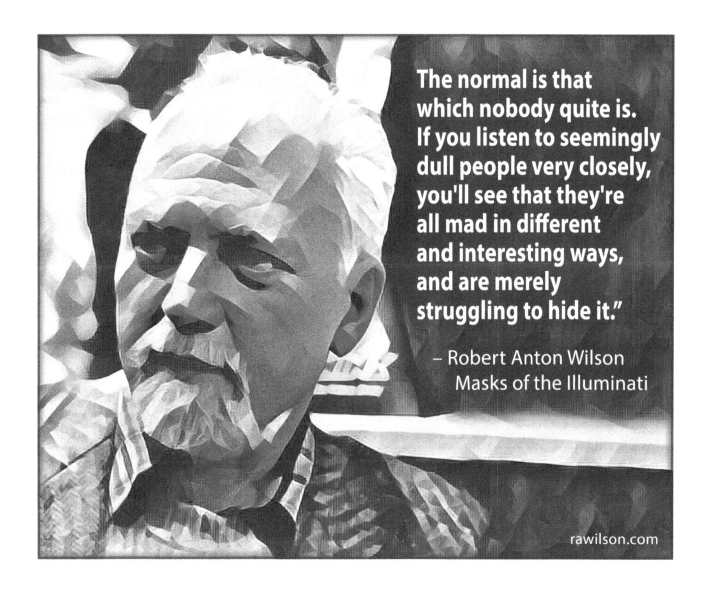

The normal is that which nobody quite is. If you listen to seemingly dull people very closely, you'll see that they're all mad in different and interesting ways, and are merely struggling to hide it."

– Robert Anton Wilson
Masks of the Illuminati

rawilson.com

Animals only suffer physical pain; humans suffer both physical pain and an additional psychological pain from the thought (verbal construct), "I should not have to suffer this."

This causes us to struggle for social progress, better medicine etc. but it also causes us to feel the same bitter sense of "injustice" or "wrongness" when there is nothing concretely that can be done to ease the pain.

In short, without language we'd have less suffering and no progress.

– Cosmic Trigger II: Down to Earth

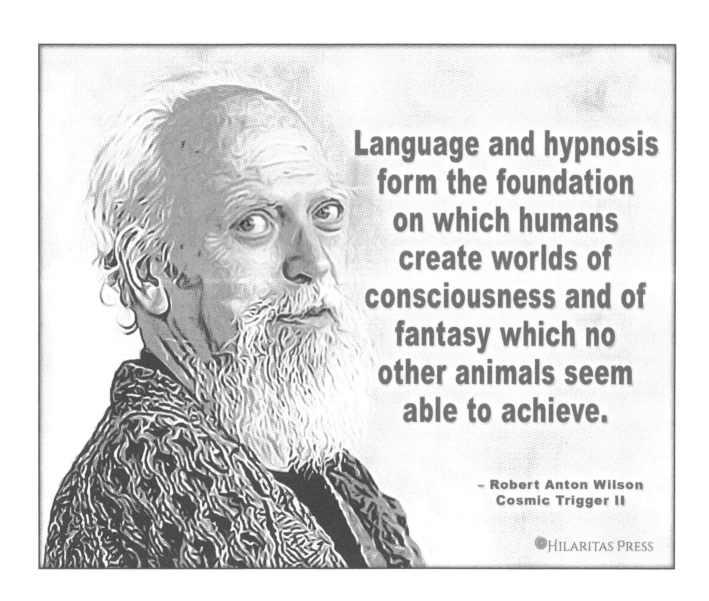

Language and hypnosis form the foundation on which humans create worlds of consciousness and of fantasy which no other animals seem able to achieve.

– Robert Anton Wilson
Cosmic Trigger II

HILARITAS PRESS

One of my favorite quotes is from T.S. Eliot: "Humility is endless." When I was in my forties I began to realize how stupid I was in my thirties, when I thought I was already an adult. And now that I'm in my fifties I can see how stupid I was in my forties. I suspect when I'm in my sixties I'll look back and see that I'm still pretty stupid right now. Humility is realism. It's the recognition of how dumb we all are and how hard it is to wake up for even a few minutes, to have even a few lucid interludes in a week.

– Natural Law, Or Don't Put A Rubber On Your Willy
And Other Writings From A Natural Outlaw

". . . I refer here to my state of ignorance in the mid 1970s, before I advanced to the more complex state of ignorance I now possess . . ."

– Robert Anton Wilson
Cosmic Trigger II: Down to Earth

HILARITAS PRESS
photo by Duncan Harvey

Although everybody in the neurological and social sciences has understood this for at least 40 or 50 years, the known techniques for curing the problem — reframing, deconditioning, getting rid of the spooks, detaching from the fixed ideas — have all had major drawbacks that notoriously prevent popularizing them. *Most of the effective techniques require hard work.* Worse yet, some not only require hard work but come from non-white cultures — from the yogis and shamans of the Third World — and the "mental imperialism" still rampant in our culture makes it impossible for most people to take seriously any discipline that doesn't have "respectable" Caucasian ancestry. (See *The Skeptical Inquirer*, any issue.)

Cosmic Trigger II: Down to Earth

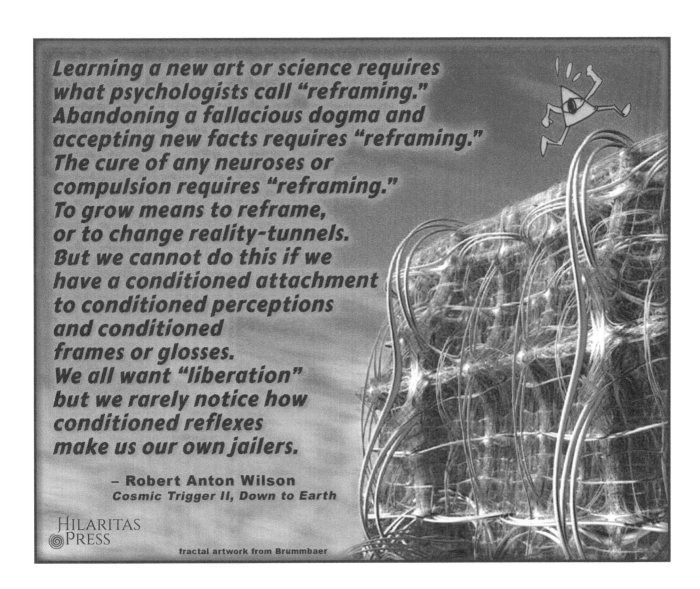

Learning a new art or science requires what psychologists call "reframing." Abandoning a fallacious dogma and accepting new facts requires "reframing." The cure of any neuroses or compulsion requires "reframing." To grow means to reframe, or to change reality-tunnels. But we cannot do this if we have a conditioned attachment to conditioned perceptions and conditioned frames or glosses. We all want "liberation" but we rarely notice how conditioned reflexes make us our own jailers.

– **Robert Anton Wilson**
Cosmic Trigger II, Down to Earth

HILARITAS
PRESS

fractal artwork from Brummbaer

Conservatives say it is dangerous to give any group too much political power. Liberals say it is dangerous to give any group too much economic power. Both are right.

– The Illuminati Papers

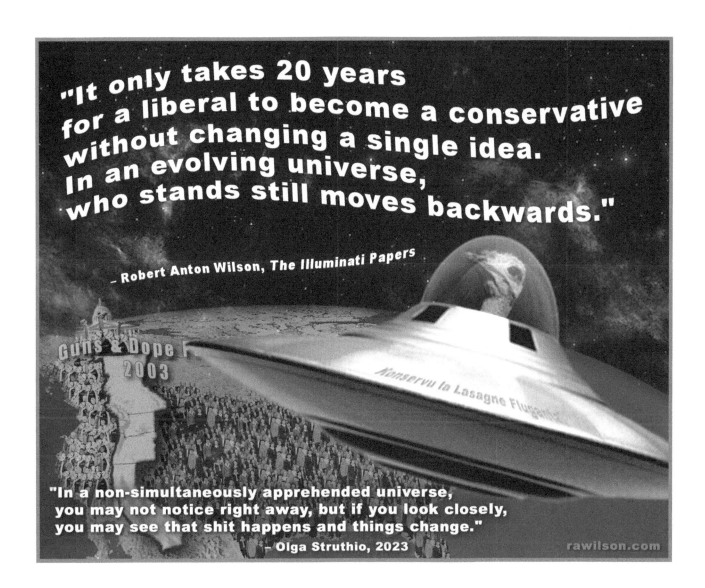

"It only takes 20 years for a liberal to become a conservative without changing a single idea. In an evolving universe, who stands still moves backwards."

— Robert Anton Wilson, *The Illuminati Papers*

Guns & Dope F...
2003

Konservu la Lasagne Flugant...

"In a non-simultaneously apprehended universe, you may not notice right away, but if you look closely, you may see that shit happens and things change."

— Olga Struthio, 2023

rawilson.com

63

Da Free John, an American guru, says you can reach Illumination by constantly asking, "Who is the One who is living me now?" Well — is it Circuit I consciousness. Circuit II ego. Circuit III mind, Circuit IV sex-role. Circuit V Gestalt- field, or a higher circuit?

– Prometheus Rising

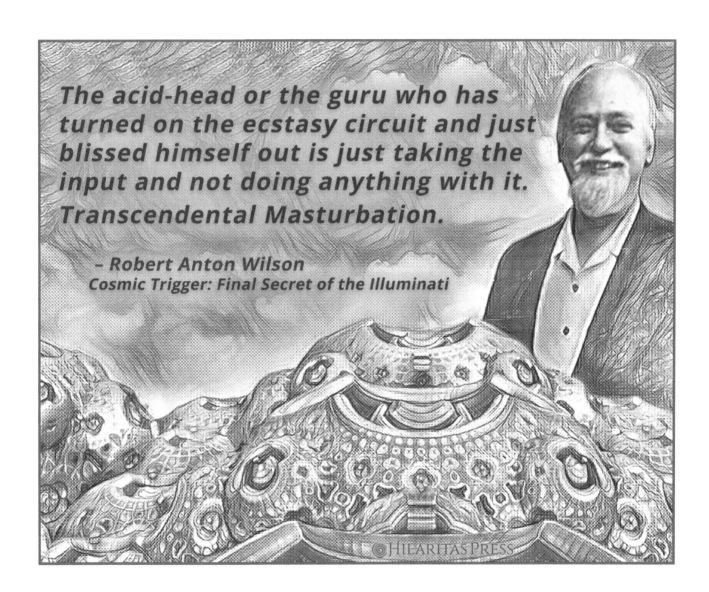

The acid-head or the guru who has turned on the ecstasy circuit and just blissed himself out is just taking the input and not doing anything with it. Transcendental Masturbation.

– Robert Anton Wilson
Cosmic Trigger: Final Secret of the Illuminati

©HILARITAS PRESS

If the world seems to be full of stupid, crazy and half-asleep people, that is because it is still dominated by Belief Systems. Whether this BS operates under the label of religion or cult or Political Correctness, it shuts off all brain functions except memorization and represents the suicide of intelligence.

– Natural Law, Or Don't Put A Rubber On Your Willy
And Other Writings From A Natural Outlaw

The totally convinced and the totally stupid have too much in common for the resemblance to be accidental.

— Robert Anton Wilson
The Historical Illuminatus Chronicles
Vol. 3, Nature's God

HILARITAS
PRESS

Political power, as a typical alpha male once said, grows out of the barrel of a gun. This is metaphorically as well as literally true. The "gun" may be symbolic and fairly abstract, consisting of ritualized social expectations ("Don't talk back to your father") or concrete in a non-violent but deadly way, e.g., the capacity to remove bio-survival necessities by cutting off the ticket supply in a Capitalist society ("One more word and I'll fire you, Bumstead!").

Under the primate second-circuit socio-biological rules, everybody tends to lie a little, to flatter or to evade displeasure, when exchanging signals with those above them in the pack-hierarchy.

Every authoritarian structure can be visualized as a pyramid with an eye on the top. This is the typical flow-chart of any government, any corporation, any Army, any bureaucracy, any mammalian pack. On each rung, participants bear a *burden of nescience* in relation to those above them. That is, they must be very, very careful that the natural sensory activities of being conscious organisms — the acts of seeing, hearing, smelling, drawing inferences from perception, etc. — are *in accord with the reality-tunnel of those above them*. This is absolutely vital; pack status (and "job security") depends on it. It is much less important — a luxury that can easily be discarded — that these perceptions be *in accord with objective fact.*

– Prometheus Rising

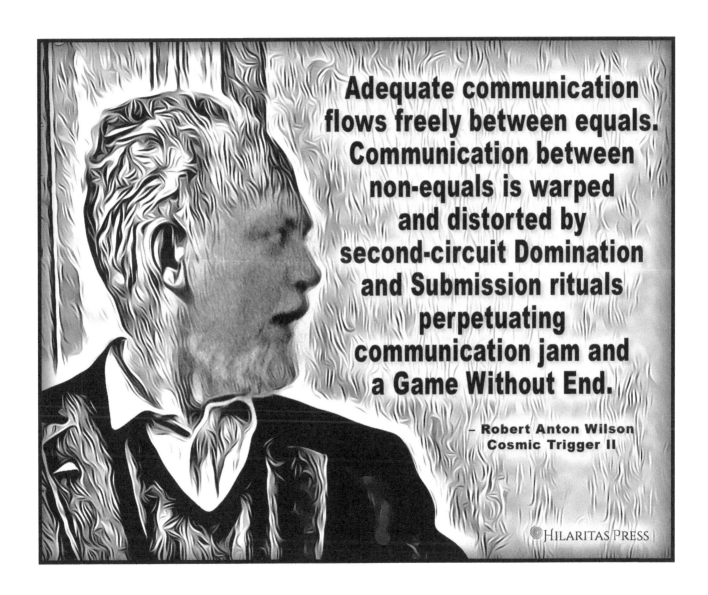

Adequate communication flows freely between equals. Communication between non-equals is warped and distorted by second-circuit Domination and Submission rituals perpetuating communication jam and a Game Without End.

– Robert Anton Wilson
Cosmic Trigger II

©Hilaritas Press

Most Terran primates did not understand the multiplex nature of causality. They tended to think everything had a single cause. This simple philosophic error was so widespread on that planet that the primates were all in the habit of giving themselves, and other primates, more credit than was deserved when things went well. This made them all inordinately conceited. They also gave themselves, and one another, more blame than was deserved when things went badly. This gave them all jumbo-sized guilt complexes. It is usually that way on primitive planets, before quantum causality is understood.

– Schrödinger's Cat Trilogy

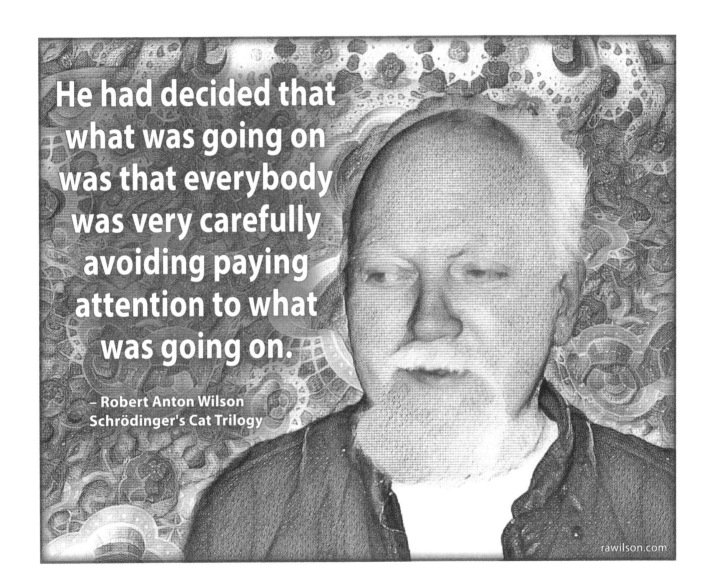

He had decided that what was going on was that everybody was very carefully avoiding paying attention to what was going on.

— Robert Anton Wilson
Schrödinger's Cat Trilogy

rawilson.com

71

. . . anyway, God has personally endorsed the GUNS AND DOPE PARTY and cursed Tsardom. He told me so, speaking through an ostrich named Olga who co-starred with Orson Welles in a thriller called The Southern Star.

Olga spoke in Orson's most sonorous and resonant voice, the one he used for Father Mapple in Moby Dick. Orson, in another second-rate villain role, spoke in a lispy, sqeeaky, very Gay, upper-class English voice, which made the character, a bandit chief, a lot more interesting.

At the climax, Olga said, looking right at the camera, "I am the Lord God. Do you believe that?"

I giggled and said, "No...I think I just took too much pain medicine..."

"Good," said Olga/Orson/Father Mapple. "I'm sick and tired of gullible fools like Dubya and Son of Sam. Just keep an open mind, old chum, and watch me rear back and work some Miracles for the Guns and Dope Party! Damn those pesky Tsarists! By the way, don't forget your promise to include 33% ostriches in your government."

Those other guys are just jealous because the Voices don't speak to them and they have to fake it!

– gunsanddopeparty.net

Olga Struthio

We all need Olga . . .
Without her, we might take ourselves –
and featherless biped politics in general –
too damned seriously, following the usual
"slippery slope" downward from Ideology
to Idiocy. We need the perspectives of
our feathered cousins, no matter how
weird they may sound at times.

— Robert Anton Wilson

rawilson.com

"*Cosmic Trigger* sparkles with humor, openness of mind, courage, understanding, tolerance. It is the epic adventure of a man who invites us to grow and change with him."

– Timothy Leary, in his introduction to
Cosmic Trigger: Final Secret of the Illuminati

After forming the Guns and Dope Party in 2003, a member of Bob's GroupMind email list wrote:

I ask: why would you promote gun-toting people who marginalize somebody like you as a silly doped up eccentric? The Charlton Heston fans are not very likely to join your party -- so what's the point?

Bob replied,

Are you sure they have the same kind of negative stereotype about us that you have about them? I'm not . . . and willing to find out by appealing to both . . .
--Guv Bob

Star Trek is a better guide to the emerging reality than anything in the *New York Review of Books*. The life-support and defense-system engineer, Scotty (circuit I), the emotional-sentimental Dr. McCoy (circuit II), the logical science-officer Mr. Spock (circuit III) and the alternately paternalistic and romantic Captain Kirk (circuit IV) are perpetually voyaging through our future neurological history and encountering circuit V, VI, VII, and VIII intelligences, however crudely presented.

In short, the various levels of consciousness and circuits we have been discussing, and illustrating, are all biochemical imprints in the evolution of the nervous system. Each imprint creates a bigger tunnel-reality. In the Sufi metaphor, the donkey on which we ride becomes a different donkey after each imprint. The metaprogrammer continually learns more and is increasingly able to be aware of itself operating. We are thus evolving to intelligence-studying-intelligence (the nervous system studying the nervous system) and are more and more capable of accelerating our own evolution.

– Cosmic Trigger: Final Secret of the Illuminati

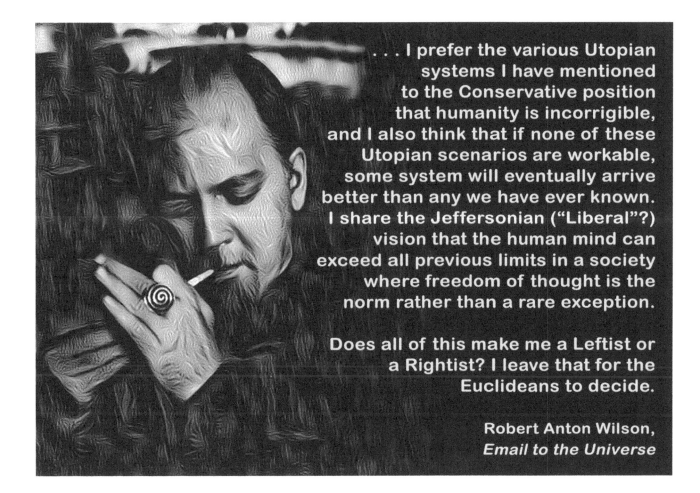

. . . I prefer the various Utopian systems I have mentioned to the Conservative position that humanity is incorrigible, and I also think that if none of these Utopian scenarios are workable, some system will eventually arrive better than any we have ever known. I share the Jeffersonian ("Liberal"?) vision that the human mind can exceed all previous limits in a society where freedom of thought is the norm rather than a rare exception.

Does all of this make me a Leftist or a Rightist? I leave that for the Euclideans to decide.

Robert Anton Wilson,
Email to the Universe

Most interesting of recent Utopias to me is that of Buckminster Fuller in which money is abolished, and computers manage the economy, programmed with a prime directive to *advantage all without disadvantaging any* — the same goal sought by the mutualist system of basing society entirely on negotiated contract.

Since I don't have the Correct Answer, I don't know which of these systems would work best in practice. I would like to see them all tried in different places, just to see what would happen.

– Email to the Universe
and other alterations of consciousness

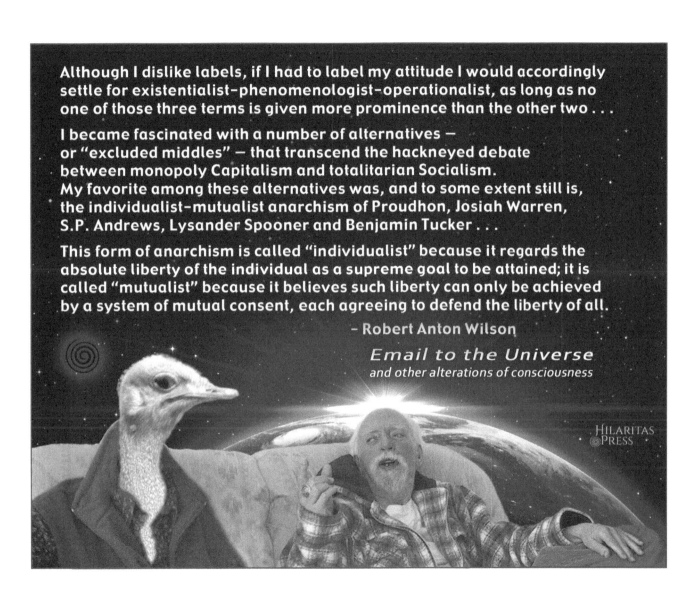

Although I dislike labels, if I had to label my attitude I would accordingly settle for existentialist–phenomenologist–operationalist, as long as no one of those three terms is given more prominence than the other two . . .

I became fascinated with a number of alternatives — or "excluded middles" — that transcend the hackneyed debate between monopoly Capitalism and totalitarian Socialism. My favorite among these alternatives was, and to some extent still is, the individualist–mutualist anarchism of Proudhon, Josiah Warren, S.P. Andrews, Lysander Spooner and Benjamin Tucker . . .

This form of anarchism is called "individualist" because it regards the absolute liberty of the individual as a supreme goal to be attained; it is called "mutualist" because it believes such liberty can only be achieved by a system of mutual consent, each agreeing to defend the liberty of all.

– Robert Anton Wilson

Email to the Universe
and other alterations of consciousness

HILARITAS
PRESS

Dating from Adorno in the 1940s, psychologists who do surveys on large groups (e.g., entering college freshpersons) have repeatedly noted a correlation between dislike of "foreign" and "exotic" foods and the "fascist" personality. A total *Gestalt* seems to exist — a behavioral/conceptual cluster of dislike of new food – dislike of "radical" ideas/racism/nationalism/sexism/xenophobia/conservatism/phobic and/ or compulsive behaviors – fascist ideologies. This cluster makes up the well-known F-Scale (F for Fascism). Where more than two of these traits appear, the probabilities indicate that most of the others will appear.

This seems to result from a *neophobic imprint in the biosurvival system.* Those with this imprint feel increasingly insecure as they move in space-time away from Mommy and "home-cooked meals." Conversely, those who like to experiment with strange and exotic foods seem to have a *neophilic imprint* and want to explore the world in many dimensions — traveling, moving from one city or country to another, studying new subjects, "playing" with ideas rather than holding rigidly to one static model of the universe.

Quantum Psychology: How Brain Software
Programs You and Your World

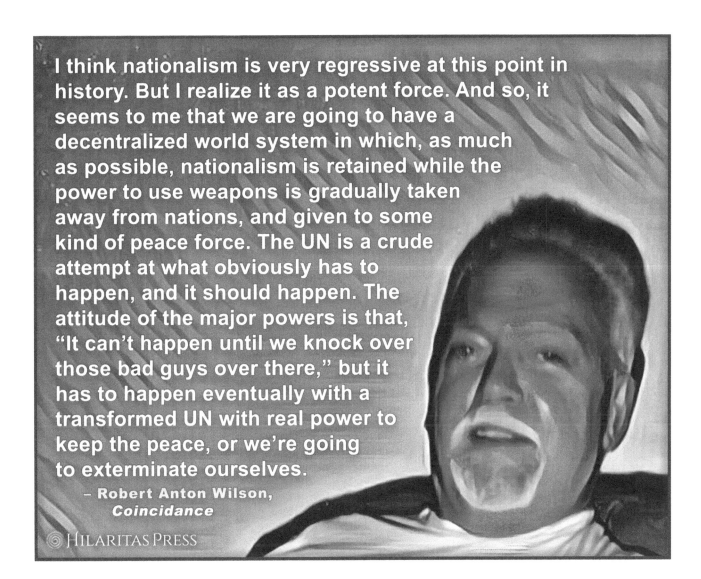

I think nationalism is very regressive at this point in history. But I realize it as a potent force. And so, it seems to me that we are going to have a decentralized world system in which, as much as possible, nationalism is retained while the power to use weapons is gradually taken away from nations, and given to some kind of peace force. The UN is a crude attempt at what obviously has to happen, and it should happen. The attitude of the major powers is that, "It can't happen until we knock over those bad guys over there," but it has to happen eventually with a transformed UN with real power to keep the peace, or we're going to exterminate ourselves.

– Robert Anton Wilson,
Coincidance

HILARITAS PRESS

. . . the reader should now be able to grasp that the "extravagant metaphors" in love poets like Vidal, Sordello, Chaucer, Shakespeare, Donne, etc., are often not a matter of flattering the lady but serious statements of a philosophy which runs directly counter to the basic assumptions of our anal-patriarchal culture. Specifically, the repeated, perfectly clear identifications of the poet's mistress with a goddess are part of the mental set, or ritual, connected with this cult. Tibetan teachers train disciples of Tantra to think of the female partner as being literally, not metaphorically, the goddess Shakti, divine partner of Shiva. The Sufis, working within the monotheistic patriarchy of Islam, could not emulate this, but made her an angel communicating between Allah and man. The witch covens made her the great mother goddess. Aleister Crowley's secret teachings, in our own century, instructed his pupils to envision her as the Egyptian star-goddess, Nuit.

When anthropologist Weston La Barre says, "Mothers make magicians; fathers, gods," he means that the magic or shamanistic trance is a return to the bliss at the breast of the all-giving mother, while religion is an anal propitiation of a fearful god who is an enlarged portrait of the punishing father. These distinctions do not always remain sharp—Tantra managed to get incorporated into the patrist framework of Hinduism, and Sufi sex-magic into the equally patrist Moslem faith of Allah. In the West, however, patriarchy became extreme; Jehovah would bode no rivals, least of all a goddess equal to himself, and the magic-matriarchal-oral cults were driven underground, masqueraded as pseudo-sciences like alchemy, or came forth only in the form of poetry.

– *Coincidance: A Head Test*

"... if the primitive matriarchy did not exist as universally as the 19th-Century theorists imagined, something much like it existed just before the dawn of recorded history in the West and Near East and coexisted with the first patriarchal civilizations for a while. The oral and gentle mother goddesses are a survival of that period, and there have been various attempts to revive its values in historical times. G. Rattray Taylor even provides a table showing the differences between the two kinds of cultures, which he calls patrist and matrist. In strict Freudian terms they are, of course, respectively, anal and oral."

Patrist (anal)	Matrist (oral)
1. Restrictive attitude toward sex	1. Permissive attitude toward sex
2. Limitation of freedom for women	2. Freedom for women
3. Women seen as inferior, sinful	3. Women accorded high status
4. Chastity more valued than welfare	4. Welfare more valued than chastity
5. Politically authoritarian	5. Politically democratic
6. Conservative: against innovation	6. Progressive: revolutionary
7. Distrust of research, inquiry	7. No distrust of research
8. Inhibition, fear of spontaneity	8. Spontaneity: exhibition
9. Deep fear of homosexuality	9. Deep fear of incest
10. Sex differences maximized (dress)	10. Sex differences minimized (dress)
11. Asceticism, fear of pleasure	11. Hedonism, pleasure welcomed
12. Father-religion	12. Mother-religion

from Robert Anton Wilson's
Coincidance

And they looked at the Vision more closely, and because they could see into the future and were all (like every intelligent entity) rabid Laurel and Hardy fans and because they were zonked on the weed, they saw that Yahweh bore the face of Oliver Hardy. All around him, below the mountain on which he lived (his world was flat), the waters rose and rose. They saw drowning men, drowning women, innocent babes sinking beneath the waves. They were ready to vomit. And then Another came and stood beside Yahweh, looking at the panorama of horrors below, and he was Yahweh's Adversary, and, stoned as they were, he looked like Stanley Laurel to them. And then Yahweh spoke, in the eternal words of Oliver Hardy: "Now look what you made me do," he said.

– Illuminatus!

Although the underground press was absolutely fundamentalist in its allegiance to the Garrison Revelations, it was also intensely gullible and eager to believe all manner of additional conspiracy theories, the weirder the better. Most Discordians, at this time, were contributors to underground newspapers all over the country. We began surfacing the Discordian Society, issuing position papers offering non-violent anarchist techniques to mutate our robot-society. One was our "PURSE" plan (Permanent Universal Rent Strike Exchange) in which everybody simply stops paying rent forever. (Can they dispossess us all into the Atlantic and Pacific?) Another was our "PUTZ" plan (Permanent Universal Tax Zap), in which everybody stops paying taxes. Along with this we planted numerous stories about the Discordian Society's aeon-old war against the sinister Illuminati. We accused everybody of being in the Illuminati — Nixon, Johnson, William Buckley, Jr., ourselves, Martian invaders, all the conspiracy buffs, everybody.

We did not regard this as a hoax or prank in the ordinary sense. We still considered it guerrilla ontology.

My personal attitude was that if the New Left wanted to live in the particular tunnel-reality of the hard-core paranoid, they had an absolute right to that neurological choice. I saw Discordianism as the Cosmic Giggle Factor, introducing so many alternative paranoias that everybody could pick a favorite, if they were inclined that way. I also hoped that some less gullible souls, overwhelmed by this embarrassment of riches, might see through the whole paranoia game and decide to mutate to a wider, funnier, more hopeful reality-map.

– Cosmic Trigger I: Final Secret of the Illuminati

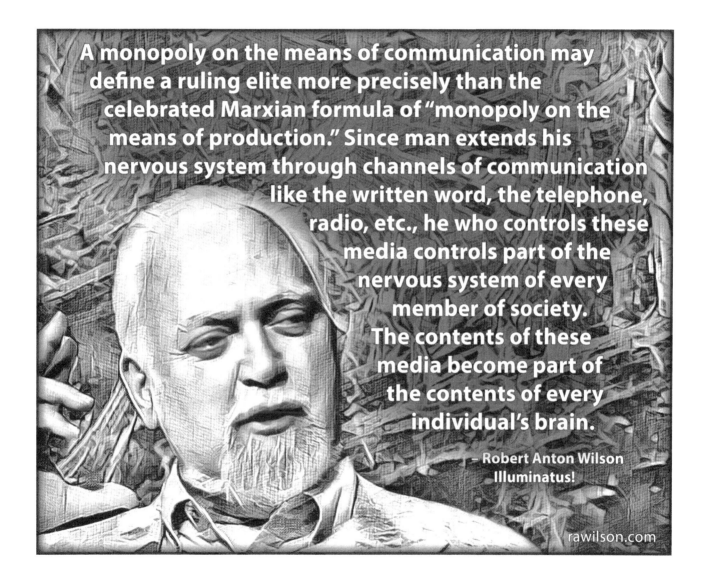

A monopoly on the means of communication may define a ruling elite more precisely than the celebrated Marxian formula of "monopoly on the means of production." Since man extends his nervous system through channels of communication like the written word, the telephone, radio, etc., he who controls these media controls part of the nervous system of every member of society. The contents of these media become part of the contents of every individual's brain.

– Robert Anton Wilson
Illuminatus!

rawilson.com

Every affinity group looks like a conspiracy from outside. Every conspiracy thinks of itself as an affinity group, and only becomes a true conspiracy in the legal sense when it creates "lies that look like truth" — when it becomes magic, or a con-game, or a cognate of the art tricks that look like "realism." Where does fraud leave off and art or entertainment begin? If you could tell worthless bonds at sight, nobody would ever buy them. In certain meditative states well-known in the Orient and among pot-heads, the difference between a "real" dollar and a counterfeit becomes obliterated; they're both just pretty designs on paper. A counterfeit dollar could even become worth more than a "real" dollar, if a popular artist put a frame around it and exhibited it in a gallery. I was in a TV documentary called "Borders" recently — which was about the vanishing of borders in our world — and when I saw the final cut, it included an artist who declared an air conditioner at the Museum of Modern Art to be a work of modern art itself and wanted credit for discovering it; I can only congratulate him for crossing more borders than I have. If I said, "game" instead of "conspiracy" throughout this interview, many sociologists would say I'm just popularizing their analysis of how society works. My novels look like melodramas part of the time and then switch over and look like black comedies, but isn't that true of politics also? If you believe somebody's war propaganda, the world is pure melodrama — the good guys versus the bad guys. If you start doubting all propaganda, the world becomes black comedy — "a darkling plain/swept by confused alarms of struggle and flight/where ignorant armies clash by night," i.e., a more violent and ugly version of the Three Stooges. I can't see things from every possible perspective, but I try to see them from enough kinky new angles that my books never degenerate into war propaganda for any of the ignorant armies that go on clashing by night.

– Cosmic Trigger II: Down to Earth

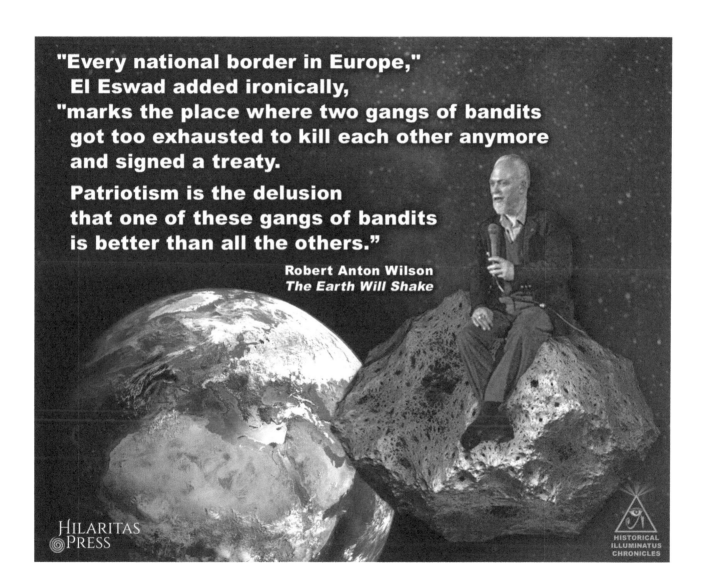

"Every national border in Europe,"
 El Eswad added ironically,
"marks the place where two gangs of bandits
 got too exhausted to kill each other anymore
 and signed a treaty.

Patriotism is the delusion
that one of these gangs of bandits
is better than all the others."

Robert Anton Wilson
The Earth Will Shake

HILARITAS
PRESS

HISTORICAL
ILLUMINATUS
CHRONICLES

World War I veterans marched on Washington, protesting the lack of promised veterans' benefits, and the Army used tanks, machine guns and bayonets to disperse them. There were more than 100 casualties.

– Cosmic Trigger II: Down to Earth

I can't see how the NRA can avoid eventually making this part of their platform: the right of the citizens to bear grenade launchers, flame-throwers, tactical missiles and nuclear weapons. If the citizens have the right to bear arms, they should have the right to bear as many arms as the government, or it's no defense against the government at all, and that whole argument is hollow.

Robert Anton Wilson
Trajectories, 1990

rawilson.com

91

After Pearl Harbor, my brother — who was 18 years older than me, and married already — received a draft notice. That night I woke up and went to the kitchen to get a drink of milk. I found my mother and my brother's wife, who normally did not get along well, drinking whiskey. Their faces were stained with tears and they were cursing President Roosevelt — I guess they were too drunk, by then, to remember that they had a rule about not using such language in front of children. They had no doubt that President Roosevelt had plotted Pearl Harbor and they were saying wild, crazy things, even threatening to vote Republican for the rest of their lives.

"It's men," my mother said. "They never grow up. They're all still boys. Playing with guns." She started to cry again.

– Cosmic Trigger II: Down to Earth

I've written a living will and it includes a paragraph stating nothing in this will may be set aside by any politician in Republican or human form contrary to my explicit instructions.
– Robert Anton Wilson

rawilson.com

93

I remember the great scene in *My Little Chickadee* where W.C. Fields is about to be hanged. As the noose is slipped about his neck, he is asked if he has any last words.

"Um, yes," he replies thoughtfully. "This will certainly teach me a lesson."

The comment is brilliant, not just on capital punishment, but on punishment per se, which never teaches any lesson except desire for revenge.

As the 1960s progressed, and the "war on drugs" escalated, our jails filled with more and more young people convicted of *desire to experiment on alterations of consciousness*. I became convinced that Mad magazine was right in claiming "the missing link between ape and civilized humanity is us."

– The Starseed Signals

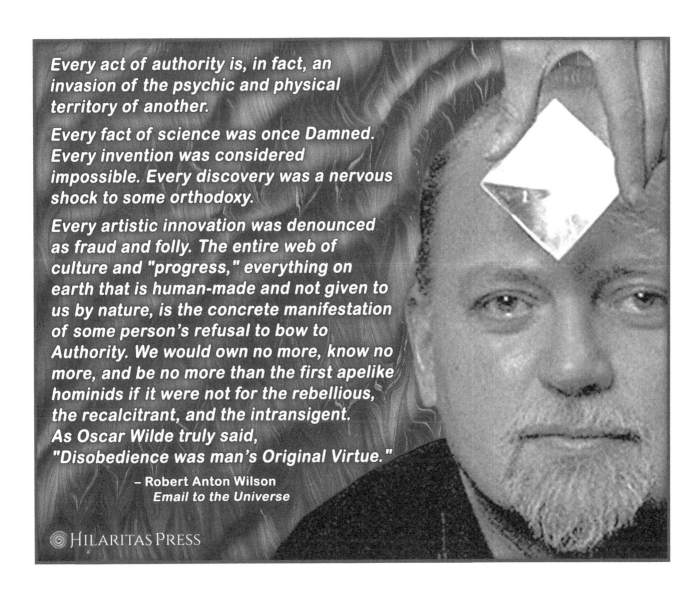

Every act of authority is, in fact, an invasion of the psychic and physical territory of another.

Every fact of science was once Damned. Every invention was considered impossible. Every discovery was a nervous shock to some orthodoxy.

Every artistic innovation was denounced as fraud and folly. The entire web of culture and "progress," everything on earth that is human-made and not given to us by nature, is the concrete manifestation of some person's refusal to bow to Authority. We would own no more, know no more, and be no more than the first apelike hominids if it were not for the rebellious, the recalcitrant, and the intransigent. As Oscar Wilde truly said, "Disobedience was man's Original Virtue."

– Robert Anton Wilson
Email to the Universe

HILARITAS PRESS

There were some Protestants in Gerritsen Beach, and they all went to a church which we kids called the "piss-in-the-pail-ian" church. Many years passed and I was developing pimples and horniness — symptoms of the increase of testosterone at puberty — before I learned that the correct name was "Episcopalian." The only Jews I knew anything about lived in Brooklyn, on Ocean Boulevard. Whether they had caused The Depression or not, everybody knew they had killed Christ. *

~•~

* I was about 30 when I heard Lenny Bruce explain this: "All my life goys have asked me why we killed Christ. What can I say? Maybe he wouldn't become a doctor. Maybe it was just one of those wild parties that got out of hand."

~•~

– Cosmic Trigger II: Down to Earth

Of all the voices attacking conformity in the 1960s, Bruce was the only one literally hounded to death, because repression can survive literally anything except a room full of people laughing at it.

– Robert Anton Wilson
Ishtar Rising
Why the Goddess Went to Hell
and What to Expect Now
That She's Returning

HILARITAS PRESS

The next link in the Net was a meeting with Dr. Timothy Leary, the man who either brainwashed a whole generation with mind-warping drugs (opinion of his enemies) or discovered how to free the mind of humanity from culturally conditioned limitations (opinion of his friends).

– Cosmic Trigger I: Final Secret Of The Illuminati

"I regard myself and my friends as the power elite. That way I don't have to worry if someone else is manipulating me. They're trying, but we're outsmarting them every step of the way. Most people want to believe somebody else is in charge. Then they don't have to take responsibility. Then they have the supreme pleasure of perpetually complaining that somebody else is in charge, and it would be better if only they were in charge. As long as I think I'm in charge, I've got nothing to complain about. I've got to take the responsibility for all of it.

How can I go on? (laughs) Well, some of us have more balls than others. I'm sixty years old. In any traditional society I would have been hanged long ago."

Robert Anton Wilson, Dedroidify Interview, 1992

rawilson.com
Photo by James Nye, 1992

From the date of first printing to the present, I have received more mail about *Cosmic Trigger* than about anything else I ever wrote, and most of this mail has been unusually intelligent and open-minded. For some reason, many readers of this book think they can write to me intimately and without fear, about subjects officially Taboo in our society. I have learned a great deal from this correspondence, and have met some wonderful new friends.

– Cosmic Trigger I: Final Secret Of The Illuminati

You should view the world as a conspiracy run by a very closely-knit group of nearly omnipotent people, and you should think of those people as yourself and your friends.

– Robert Anton Wilson

rawilson.com

None of the investigative agencies charged with bringing hard evidence into court, however, have ever found traces of any of the Really Big Conspiracies that most "conspiracy buffs" believe in. This, of course, only proves one thing to the true conspiriologist: The major conspiracies really do have almost universal power, because the investigating agencies themselves "are part of the cover-up." Against that kind of logic, the gods themselves contend in vain.

– Everything Is Under Control:
Conspiracies, Cults, and Cover-ups

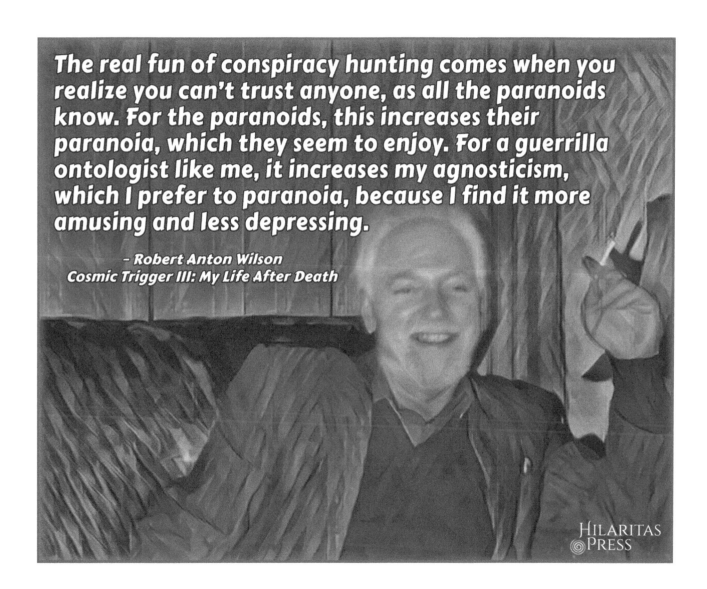

The real fun of conspiracy hunting comes when you realize you can't trust anyone, as all the paranoids know. For the paranoids, this increases their paranoia, which they seem to enjoy. For a guerrilla ontologist like me, it increases my agnosticism, which I prefer to paranoia, because I find it more amusing and less depressing.

- Robert Anton Wilson
Cosmic Trigger III: My Life After Death

HILARITAS PRESS

Discordians worship a female divinity, but say She is crazy. Her name, in fact, is Eris, and the ancient Greeks knew her as the Goddess of Chaos; Discordians claim she is also the Goddess of Confusion, Discord and Bureaucracy. The Discordian orthodoxy, headed by "Ho Chih Zen" (real name, Kerry Thornley), claims this was revealed by a miraculous talking chimpanzee, who appeared in a bowling alley in Yorba Linda, California in 1957. The POEE sect flatly rejects this, says it is superstitious nonsense intended to attract the gullible, and proves the existence of Eris by Five Proofs, which are all logical monstrosities and reduce actually to One Proof—namely, "If Eris doesn't exist, who put all the Chaos in this universe, you damned atheist?"

– Coincidance: A Head Test

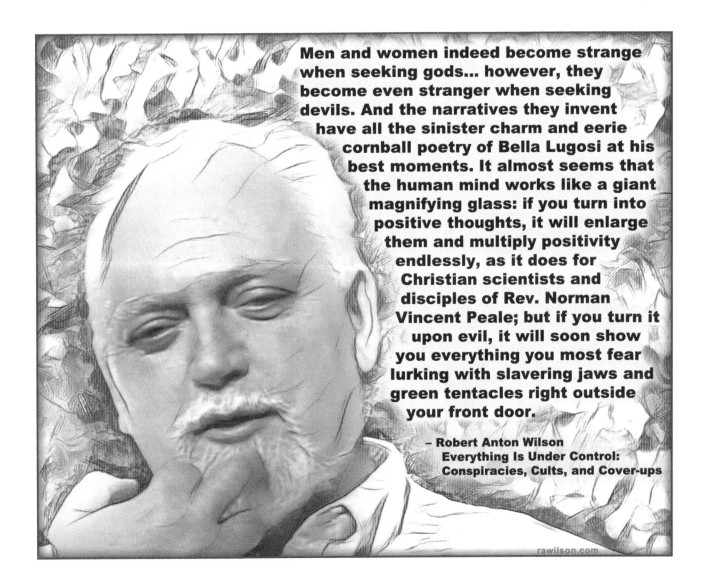

Men and women indeed become strange when seeking gods... however, they become even stranger when seeking devils. And the narratives they invent have all the sinister charm and eerie cornball poetry of Bella Lugosi at his best moments. It almost seems that the human mind works like a giant magnifying glass: if you turn into positive thoughts, it will enlarge them and multiply positivity endlessly, as it does for Christian scientists and disciples of Rev. Norman Vincent Peale; but if you turn it upon evil, it will soon show you everything you most fear lurking with slavering jaws and green tentacles right outside your front door.

– Robert Anton Wilson
Everything Is Under Control:
Conspiracies, Cults, and Cover-ups

rawilson.com

Transactional psychology reveals that perceptions begin always in the "*maybe*" state. I walk down the street and see good old Joe half a block away. If I haven't studied brain science, I feel sure that the Joe I see "is really" there, and I feel quite surprised when the figure comes closer and I now see a man who only resembles good old Joe slightly. My perception contained a "*maybe*" but, conditioned by Aristotelian logic, I ignored this and my conception leaped to premature certainty. (This description has been simplified for logical clarity. In experience, the feedback loop *from perception to conception and back to perception* operates so quickly, that we "see" what we think we should see and the *maybe* virtually never registers – until we re-train ourselves to register it.)

– Coincidance: A Head Test

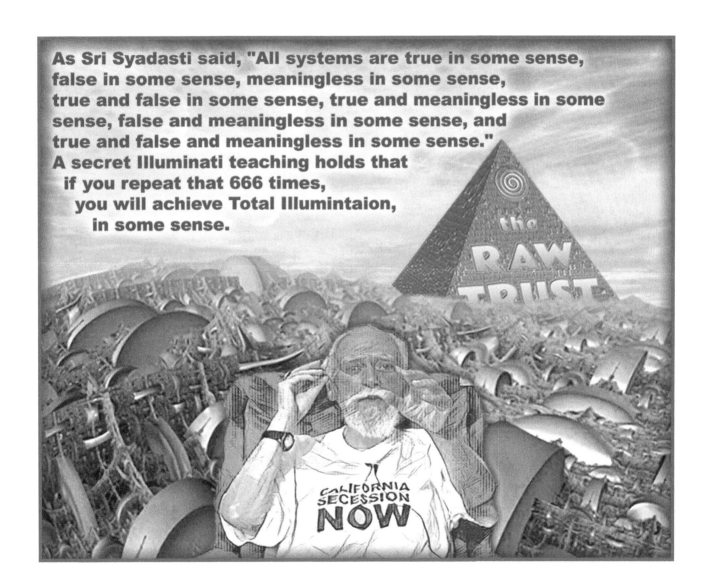

As Sri Syadasti said, "All systems are true in some sense, false in some sense, meaningless in some sense, true and false in some sense, true and meaningless in some sense, false and meaningless in some sense, and true and false and meaningless in some sense." A secret Illuminati teaching holds that if you repeat that 666 times, you will achieve Total Illumintaion, in some sense.

. . . if I were interested in entering ordinary politics, in the framework of the rules of ordinary history, I would follow Rothbard's advice, "shut up" (as he urges) about my philosophical doubts, and pretend to the kind of passion and dogmatic belief that historically always leads to political success. In my view, however, such passionate dogmatism usually makes people stupid – Koestler called it "deliberate stupidity" – and it often makes them blindly cruel. It even appears to some of us that *passionate belief* can justly be called the principle reason politics remains such a depressing, paleolithic and murderous spectacle. That is why I am not interested in *entering* politics at all, but only in satirizing and undermining it, so that others may see it as I do, come to their senses, and grow reasonably pragmatic, a bit more skeptical and relatively sane and peaceful; hence, I will *not* shut up. Sorry, Professor Rothbard.

– Natural Law, Or Don't Put A Rubber On Your Willy
And Other Writings From A Natural Outlaw

Then there's the third problem where some people are not stupid, and they're not full of shit, they're just fucking crazy.

Bill Gates, he's not stupid, obviously. You can't be stupid and get that rich. He's full of shit.

Donald Trump, on the other hand, is fucking crazy.

– Robert Anton Wilson

rawilson.com

The chief fault of most academic theoreticians of postmodernism, as Gross and Levitt emphasize, lies in never applying perspectivism to themselves — i.e., in holding an oxymoronic position that always implies "everything is relative except my own dogmas." I do not make that error habitually, and I like to think I never make it at all. (I sure *hope* not, but as a Cosmic Schmuck, I assume I have slipped into it on occasion.)

– Cosmic Trigger III: My Life After Death

if you NEVER suspect that you might think or act like a Cosmic Schmuck, you will remain a Cosmic Schmuck forever
- Robert Anton Wilson

Well, in the first place I hope to get my medicine so my leg won't go on hurting the way it's been since they cut off my supply. That is the most important and immediate existential fact, I am in Pain. I want medicine.

The second reason I'm here, I happen to believe in States Rights. I believe in the 10th Amendment, which most people have never heard of. If you look in the back of your dictionary you'll find a document called the US Constitution. It has nothing to do with the way this government is operating under George Bush – it's the way it's supposed to operate. And the 10th Amendment says that all powers not delegated to the federal government are reserved to the states respectively, or to the people. Now the state of California, and the people of California, are behind me and the federal government has no right to condemn me to a life of constant pain, which is what they are trying to do. I don't know what kind of sadistic son of a bitch George Bush is, why he wants to leave people in pain like this. I don't approve of it. I don't like it, and I'm ready to fight for my right to be free of pain.

If you are going to be in pain most of the day, you are not going to enjoy your life much. And if George Bush insists that God has appointed him to ensure that I spend the rest of my life in pain without any relief, then I say, "Fuck you, George Bush, you should have these pains in your goddamn legs.

I'm a Buddhist most of the time, but today I'm too angry to be a Buddhist. I'll get back to being a Buddhist tomorrow.

. . . I'm sorry for my bitterness against George Bush. He is equally empty, equally blessed, and equally a coming Buddha. The problem is the asshole doesn't know it.

– Santa Cruz protest against the War on Some Drugs,
September 18, 2002

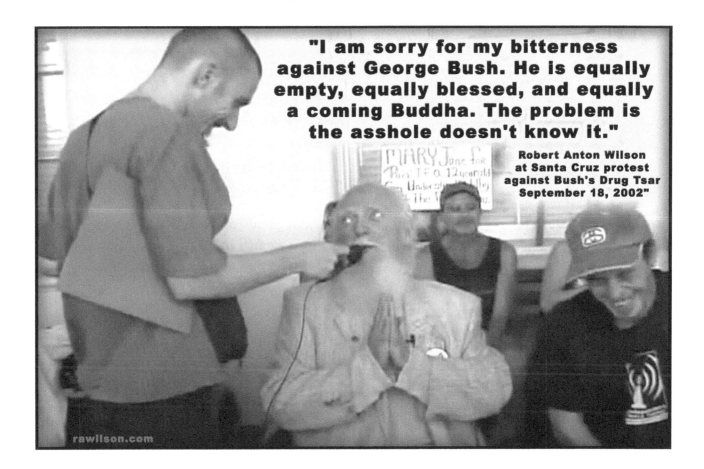

"I am sorry for my bitterness against George Bush. He is equally empty, equally blessed, and equally a coming Buddha. The problem is the asshole doesn't know it."

Robert Anton Wilson at Santa Cruz protest against Bush's Drug Tsar September 18, 2002"

rawilson.com

Q: Since you believe that the universe is indifferent, why are you an optimist?

A: It may have genetic origins — some of us bounce up again no matter what we get hit with — but as far as I can rationalize it, nobody knows the future, so choosing between pessimism and optimism depends on temperament as much as probabilities.

– Email to the Universe:
and other alterations of consciousness

Analoculectemy -- the little-known operation in which the surgeon enters through the anus and scrapes the back of the eye. Hazardous and delicate work, but absolutely necessary to correct the shitty outlook on life some people have.

– RAW quote from a GroupMind email, 1998

rawilson.com

115

Once I broke loose from the employee role and became self-supporting as a writer, the "horrors of capitalism" seemed less ghoulish to me, since I no longer had to face them every day. (As Shakespeare said, we can all bear a toothache philosophically, except the pore bloke wot's got it.) I prefer to live in Europe rather than pay taxes to build more of Mr. Reagan's goddam nuclear missiles, but I enjoy visiting the U.S. regularly for intellectual stimulation.

– Email to the Universe:
and other alterations of consciousness

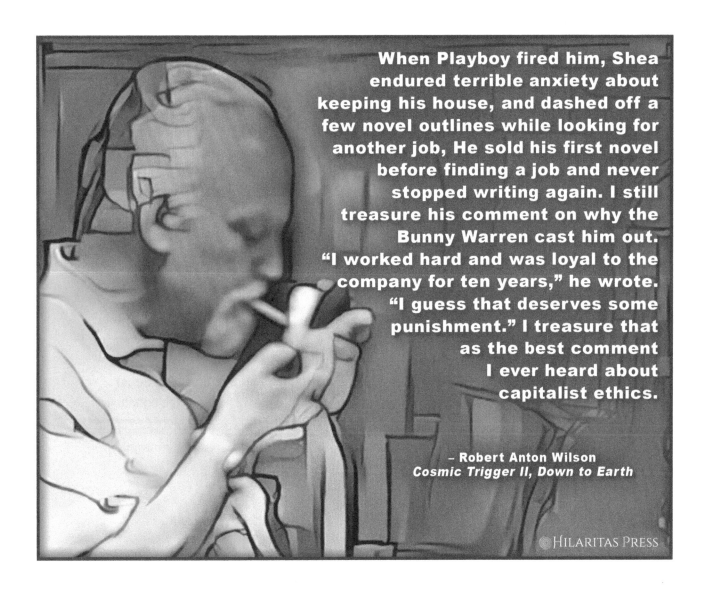

When Playboy fired him, Shea endured terrible anxiety about keeping his house, and dashed off a few novel outlines while looking for another job, He sold his first novel before finding a job and never stopped writing again. I still treasure his comment on why the Bunny Warren cast him out. "I worked hard and was loyal to the company for ten years," he wrote. "I guess that deserves some punishment." I treasure that as the best comment I ever heard about capitalist ethics.

– Robert Anton Wilson
Cosmic Trigger II, Down to Earth

© HILARITAS PRESS

117

According to the corporate media, which allows all shades of opinion from the far right to the middle-of-the road, America has vicious enemies on all continents (except maybe Antarctica). These Evildoers, driven by Satan, want to destroy us and take all we own.

Hence, by this analysis, our president must have no compunction about spilling blood; in short, like it or not, he must have the soul – or soullessness – of a serial killer.

A rival "leftish" view, banned from the corporate media but widely available on Internet, holds that the world does not consist entirely of endless enemies, but does contain many, many peoples who want to get out from under the heel of the IMF, the World Bank and the multi-nationals. "Our" government, in this view, actually belongs not to us but to these giant money-cows, who finance the two major parties and ensure that no third party ever gets decent coverage in their media. The government then acts as Company Cop for the rich, suppressing all attempts at rebellion or national liberation, etc. Thus, once again, *via* a dissenting ideology, we arrive at the conclusion that the president must think, feel and act like a serial killer.

– TSOG: The Thing That Ate The Constitution

"the corporate media...
allows all shades of opinion
from the far right to the
middle-of-the road"

– TSOG
The Thing That
Ate the Constitution

Robert Anton Wilson

HILARITAS
©PRESS

Coming from a working class family, I could never have much sympathy for the kind of Conservatism you find in America in this century. (I do have a deep respect for the classic Libertarian Conservatives of the 18th Century, especially Edmund Burke and John Adams.)

– Email to the Universe:
and other alterations of consciousness

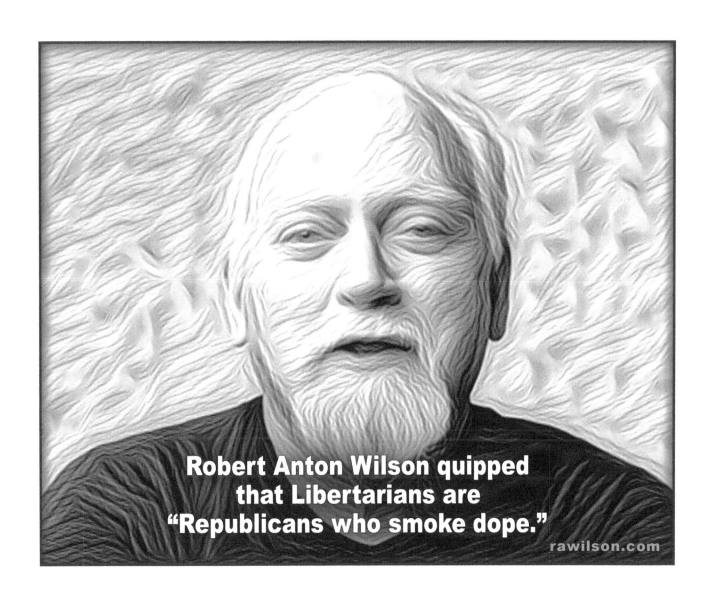

Robert Anton Wilson quipped that Libertarians are "Republicans who smoke dope."

rawilson.com

As an investigative journalist in the US, I met many members of all these cults or sects. I have found them to be above-average in intelligence and education, mostly young (average age is under 30, although some over-40s do crop up) and very erudite in anthropology, history of religion and, especially, science-fiction. Typically, they attend science-fiction conventions even more devoutly than the services or celebrations of their churches. Many of them are in the computer industry, and others in entertainment, the arts, and Academia. They frequently belong to two or more of these sects simultaneously and may also be involved in some Oriental mystical system on the side. An overwhelming majority of them also belong to the Society for Creative Anachronism, which holds "fairs" in many parts of the US at which members dress and act like persons from past centuries or from the future and everybody creates his or her own separate reality-tunnel. They are usually in favour of both ecology and technology – "appropriate technology" is one of their buzz-words, followed by "synergy" and "holism." When asked how serious they are, they usually say something to the effect that humans need some religion and they are trying to create a relativistic religion for a scientific age.

Malaclypse the Younger states it this way, "We are not engaged in a complicated joke disguised as a new religion. We are engaged in a new religion disguised as a complicated joke."

– Coincidance: A Head Test

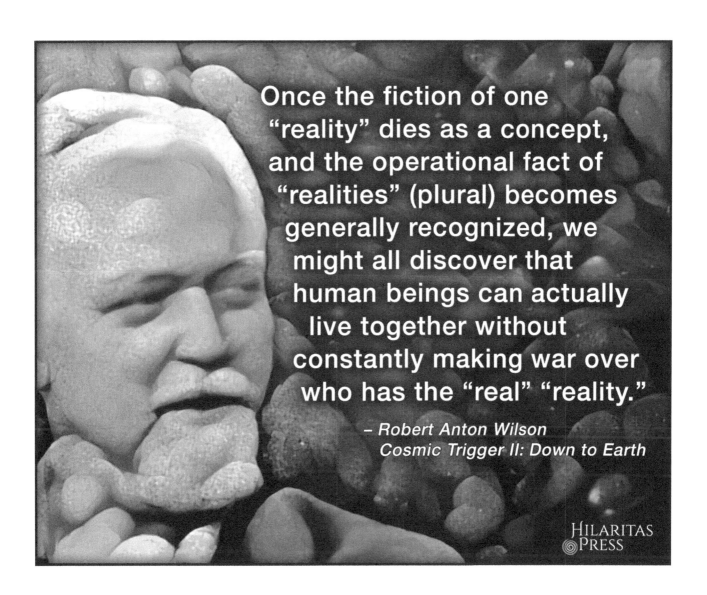

Once the fiction of one "reality" dies as a concept, and the operational fact of "realities" (plural) becomes generally recognized, we might all discover that human beings can actually live together without constantly making war over who has the "real" "reality."

– Robert Anton Wilson
Cosmic Trigger II: Down to Earth

HILARITAS PRESS

123

Karma, in the original Buddhist scriptures, *is* a blind machine; in fact, it is functionally identical with the scientific concept of natural law. Sentimental ethical ideas about justice being built into the machine, so that those who do evil in one life are punished for it in another life, were added later by theologians reasoning from their own moralistic prejudices. Buddha simply indicated that all the cruelties and injustices of the past are still active: their effects are always being felt. Similarly, he explained, all the good of the past, all the kindness and patience and love of decent people is also still being felt.

Since most humans are still controlled by fairly robotic reflexes, the bad energy of the past far outweighs the good, and the tendency of the wheel is to keep moving in the same terrible direction, violence breeding more violence, hatred breeding more hatred, war breeding more war. The only way to "stop the wheel" is to *stop it inside yourself*, by giving up bad energy and concentrating on the positive. This is by no means easy, but once you understand what Gurdjieff called "the horror of our situation," you have no choice but to try, and to keep on trying.

– Cosmic Trigger I: Final Secret Of The Illuminati

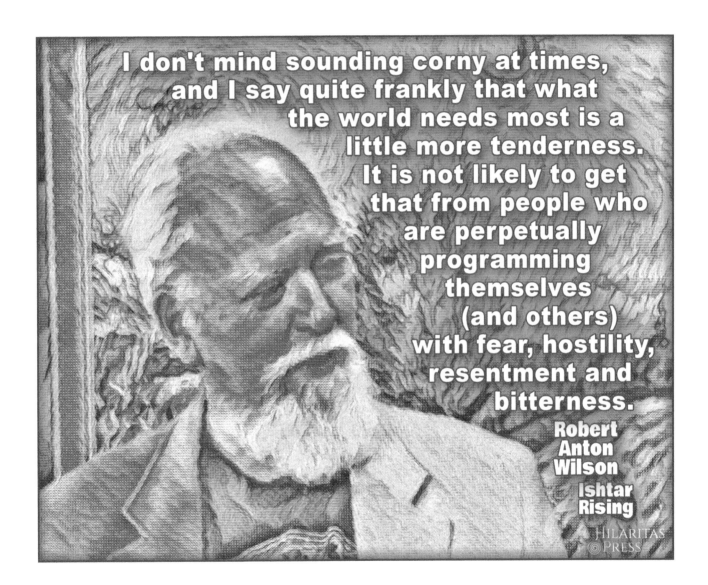

I don't mind sounding corny at times, and I say quite frankly that what the world needs most is a little more tenderness. It is not likely to get that from people who are perpetually programming themselves (and others) with fear, hostility, resentment and bitterness.

Robert Anton Wilson

Ishtar Rising

125

And I think it is curious that "ESP" is hallucinatory in the Buddhist reality tunnel as well as in the Fundamentalist Materialist reality tunnel, although for different reasons.

To the Fundamentalist, "things" have a "real existence" and "real separation" in "real space" and "real time," and therefore "my" "mind" is localized in "my" "head" and cannot make any link with "another" "mind" if they are truly "separated" in "space" and "time."

To the Buddhist, as to Schrödinger, the sum total of all "minds" is one, and no separation is "real." Hence, so-called "ESP" does not exist as a thing in itself or a "transmission" between "minds"; instead so-called "ESP" is just a partial awakening from the illusion that makes us believe in "separations." Such a partial awakening, to the Buddhist, remains in the area of hallucination, because it still assumes the "minds" are "real" and the "separation" is "real."

The New Inquisition
Irrational Rationalism and the Citadel of Science

The only sensible goal, then, is to try to build a reality-tunnel for next week that is bigger, funnier, sexier, more optimistic and generally less boring than any previous reality-tunnel.

Robert Anton Wilson
Prometheus Rising

Robert Anton Wilson
with Scott Apel
rawilson.com

Sometime in the mid 1950s, when I was still working as an engineering aide, I discovered that radio drama was not dead — at least on one New York FM station. In England, the competition created by TV drama had not reduced radio to endless music and talk shows; they were still doing dramas, and this New York station was rebroadcasting them. Among them was "The Lives of Harry Lime," starring Orson Welles — who, of course, also directed. The Great Round One also occasionally wrote some of the scripts, but a stable of writers did most of the stories and, after a while, I began to notice that the yarns I liked best were attributed to one Arlen Riley.

– *Cosmic Trigger II: Down to Earth*

Two Emails from Bob . . .

Arlen died peacefully in her sleep last night.
I'll be back on line when I feel ready.
Don't worry about me.
bob
Coinnigh an lasagne in airde!   May 22, 1999

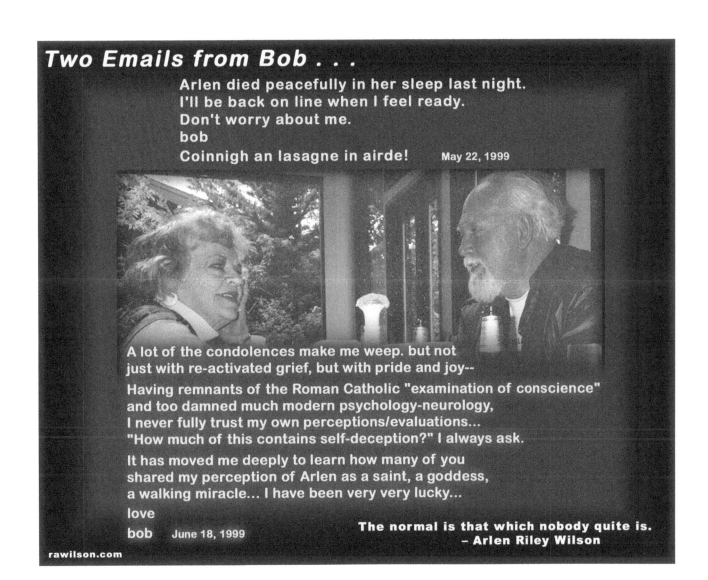

A lot of the condolences make me weep. but not
just with re-activated grief, but with pride and joy--

Having remnants of the Roman Catholic "examination of conscience"
and too damned much modern psychology-neurology,
I never fully trust my own perceptions/evaluations...
"How much of this contains self-deception?" I always ask.

It has moved me deeply to learn how many of you
shared my perception of Arlen as a saint, a goddess,
a walking miracle... I have been very very lucky...

love

bob   June 18, 1999

The normal is that which nobody quite is.
– Arlen Riley Wilson

"He taught us all that 'the universe contains a maybe.' So maybe there is an afterlife, and maybe Bob's consciousness is hovering around all of us who were touched by his words and his presence all these years. And if that's the case, I'm sure he'd like to see you do something strange and irreverent — and yet beautiful — in his honor."

– from Paul Krassner's afterword for
Email to the Universe, and other alterations of consciousness

Bob and Arlen travel in the inter-dimensional Space Cab

Arlen had a conversation with Tim, in which she expressed gratitude for the example he had given us during the last three years of his confinement. "You convinced us that it is possible to transcend suffering," she said, "and that helped us more than anything else in the first weeks after Luna's death."

Tim said, "That's the whole point of all my work on brain change!" He hugged her excitedly. "That's it! You've got it! *Positive energy is as real as gravity.* I've felt it."

– Cosmic Trigger I: Final Secret Of The Illuminati

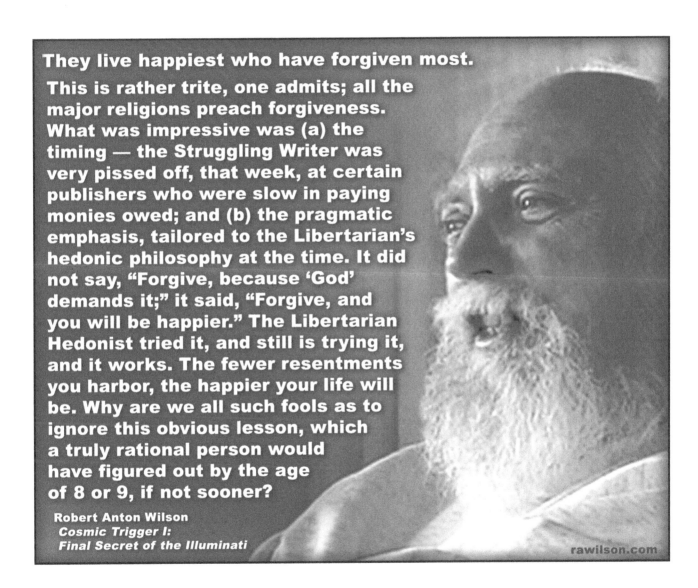

They live happiest who have forgiven most.

This is rather trite, one admits; all the major religions preach forgiveness. What was impressive was (a) the timing — the Struggling Writer was very pissed off, that week, at certain publishers who were slow in paying monies owed; and (b) the pragmatic emphasis, tailored to the Libertarian's hedonic philosophy at the time. It did not say, "Forgive, because 'God' demands it;" it said, "Forgive, and you will be happier." The Libertarian Hedonist tried it, and still is trying it, and it works. The fewer resentments you harbor, the happier your life will be. Why are we all such fools as to ignore this obvious lesson, which a truly rational person would have figured out by the age of 8 or 9, if not sooner?

Robert Anton Wilson
Cosmic Trigger I:
Final Secret of the Illuminati

rawilson.com

133

Traits are not naturally selected only for individual survival, as Darwin thought. Some are selected for species survival. Preprogrammed death was an unthinkable concept when we regarded the individual as our monad; how could natural selection produce such a genetic program, if selection is only for the advantage of the individual? But if some traits are for the advantage of the group, and for group evolution, it all falls into place. Throw out the '73 models, bring in the '74 models. Once again, I found Dr. Leary and Alan Watts, with their holistic trans-ego concepts, very helpful in firming-up my thought.

– The Starseed Signals

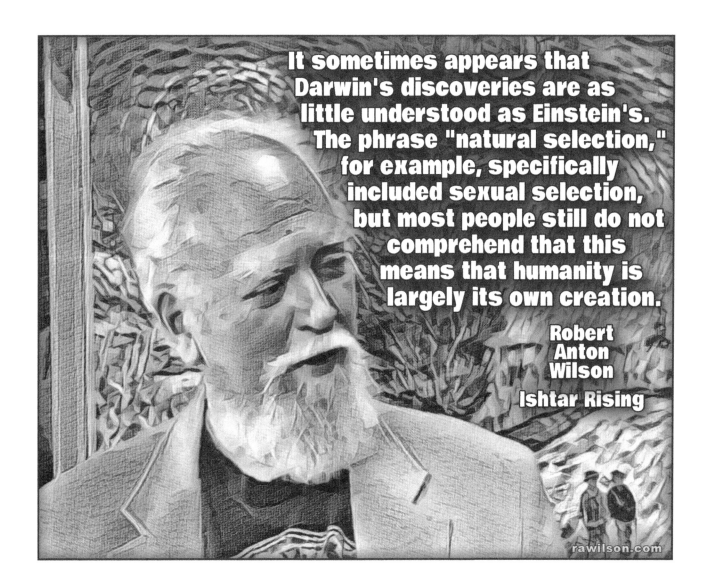

It sometimes appears that Darwin's discoveries are as little understood as Einstein's. The phrase "natural selection," for example, specifically included sexual selection, but most people still do not comprehend that this means that humanity is largely its own creation.

Robert Anton Wilson

Ishtar Rising

rawilson.com

135

Q: Would I be right in saying you probably lean more toward the libertarian form of anarchism than the classical leftist variety?

A: My trajectory is perpendicular to the left-right axis of terrestrial politics. I put some of my deepest idealism into both the Leftwing anarchism of Simon Moon and the Rightwing anarchism of Hagbard Celine in *Illuminatus!,* but I am detached from both on another level.

Politics consists of *demands*, disguised or rationalized by pseudo philosophies or bogus "social sciences" (ideologies). The disguise seems an absurdity to me and "should be" removed. *Make your demand explicit.* My emphasis is on whatever will make extraterrestrial migration possible — the sooner the better. I want to get the hell off Earth for the same reasons my ancestors left Europe: freedom is found on the expanding, pioneering perimeter, never inside the centralized State.*

~•~

* Afterthought 2004: I no longer even call myself an anarchist, since that kind of society seems much more far-off and dreamy than it did before 2000. With Bozo in the Oval Office, I would settle for a return to old-fashioned constitutional democracy. That seems pretty damned radical right now, doesn't it?

~•~

– Email to the Universe:
and other alterations of consciousness

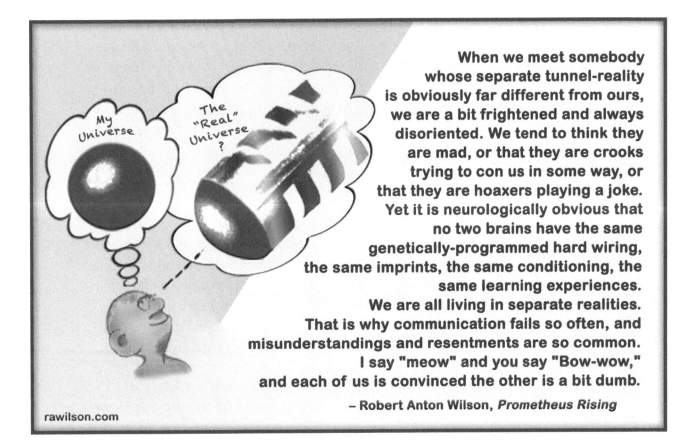

When we meet somebody whose separate tunnel-reality is obviously far different from ours, we are a bit frightened and always disoriented. We tend to think they are mad, or that they are crooks trying to con us in some way, or that they are hoaxers playing a joke. Yet it is neurologically obvious that no two brains have the same genetically-programmed hard wiring, the same imprints, the same conditioning, the same learning experiences. We are all living in separate realities. That is why communication fails so often, and misunderstandings and resentments are so common. I say "meow" and you say "Bow-wow," and each of us is convinced the other is a bit dumb.

— Robert Anton Wilson, *Prometheus Rising*

137

My polemics against Materialist Fundamentalism in *The New Inquisition* and the Aristotelian mystique of "natural law" (shared by Thomists and some Libertarians) in my *Natural Law; or, Don't Put a Rubber On Your Willy* are both based on this existentialist-phenomenologist choice that I will "believe" in — or gamble on — human experience, with all its muddle and uncertainty, more than I will ever "believe" in capitalized Abstractions and "general principles."

– Email to the Universe:
and other alterations of consciousness

But the games Joyce played — and the games played by Welles, and M.C. Escher, and Borges, and Pynchon, and a lot of our current post-modernists — while just as cute as Doyle's games, have a serious side, just like cutting-edge science and philosophy, which have also encountered Uncertainty. A Final Answer seems impossible, to post-modern artists as to current philosophers and most scientists (except Gross and Levitt.). *Ergo*, the postmodern artist now offers us, not the Problem Solved, but the Problem as Puzzle, for each of us to work at solving, as long as it continues to amuse (or annoy) us.

– Cosmic Trigger III: My Life After Death

139

M. de Selby greeted me warmly, as ever. I noticed that he looked older and grayer than he had when I last visited, and then with a faint shock realized that I also looked older and grayer. So subtly does the Ancient Enemy creep up on all of us . . .

We had some Portuguese Espresso and enjoyed some hash mixed with tobacco — a Continental custom that all the cancer warnings in the world hasn't abolished yet. You have to go to North Africa, or come back to the States, to find straight hash without nicotine poison added.

De Selby reacted with caution when I mentioned my researches into the murky Priory of Sion. "Ah, *oui*," he said dubiously. "Everybody wants to know more about them, except me. I'd rather know less, thank you. Some things should not allow themselves to become known, I think . . ."

– *Cosmic Trigger III: My Life After Death*

De Selby defines "existence" (he did not believe in "the universe" as an object) as "the sum total of such states as encountered and endured, before magnification or exaggeration by the instinct to gossip."

– Robert Anton Wilson
The Widow's Son

I wrote back, but remained mum about Sirius. Instead, just for the hell of it, I used my official Discordian Society letterhead. The stationery bears the imprint of the Joshua Norton Cabal, this being a Cabal of the Discordian Society located in the Bay Area — other Cabals including the Tactile Temple of Eris Erotic in Los Angeles, the Colorado Encrustation in Denver, the John Dillinger Died for You Society in Chicago, etc. Timothy, however, seems to have thought Joshua Norton Cabal was the name of a living person. Actually, Joshua Norton — or Norton I, as he preferred — was a San Franciscan of the last century who elected himself Emperor of the United States and Protector of Mexico. Bay Area historians still argue as to whether Norton was a psychotic or a clever con-man; in any event, he was "humored" by the citizenry of the time and, in effect, lived like an Emperor. As Greg Hill, co-founder of Discordianism, has written, "Everybody understands Mickey Mouse. Few understand Herman Hesse. Hardly anybody understands Einstein. And nobody understands Emperor Norton." (The Discordian Society, we repeat again, is not a complicated joke disguised as a new religion but really a new religion disguised as a complicated joke.)

Cosmic Trigger I: Final Secret of the Illuminati

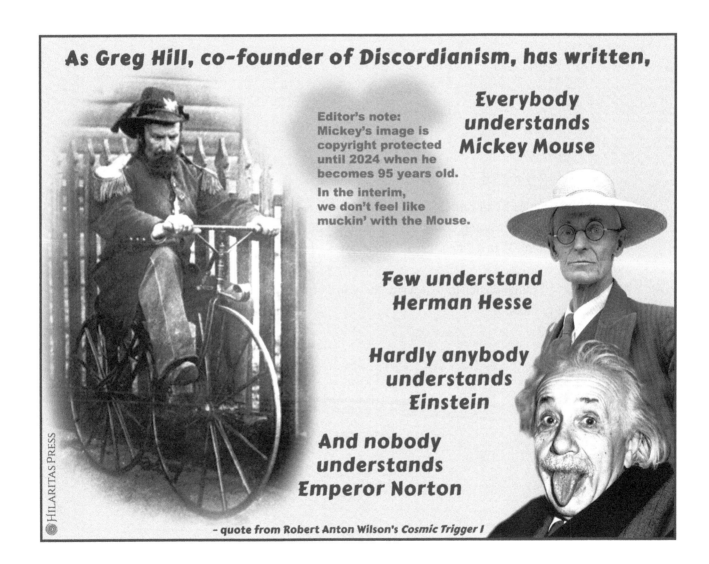

As Greg Hill, co-founder of Discordianism, has written,

Editor's note: Mickey's image is copyright protected until 2024 when he becomes 95 years old.

In the interim, we don't feel like muckin' with the Mouse.

Everybody understands Mickey Mouse

Few understand Herman Hesse

Hardly anybody understands Einstein

And nobody understands Emperor Norton

- quote from Robert Anton Wilson's *Cosmic Trigger I*

143

As far back as I can remember, I wanted to be a storyteller. When I was 8 years old, I started drawing comic strips, which I circulated among other kids in the neighborhood. When I was 12, I "discovered" that there were books made up of nothing but words!

It seemed much easier to just write the words rather than having to do the drawings to accompany them.

– Email to the Universe:
and other alterations of consciousness

By 1982, Saxon said, the whole economy would collapse. "Millions of taxpayers will be unemployed . . . Millions who are now on Valium or other tranquilizers will go insane when they cannot get more. Drug addicts (will) swarm over pharmacies looking for dope, ruining everything they don't steal . . ." We will be helpless against Russian attack because "our politicians have so devoted themselves to nurturing . . . incompetent dependents that further industrialization to put our nation on a war footing will be unaffordable. Even if it were not, our present union-spoiled and demanding work force cannot be expected to perform the way our parents did in the war plants of the late 1930s and early 1940s." The only solution, Saxon informs us, is to buy farms, order his books on how to kill people efficiently, and stockpile every type of weaponry, to fight off the "drooling imbeciles and parasites" who will flee the doomed cities and try to steal your crops.

Mr. Saxon believed that these are *objective predictions* based on hard "*laws*" of sociology and economics which he learned from the writings of Ms. Ayn Rand. He did not believe that this apocalyptical reality tunnel in which he lives is in any way an *artistic creation* expressing his own emotional anxieties and hostilities.

– Prometheus Rising

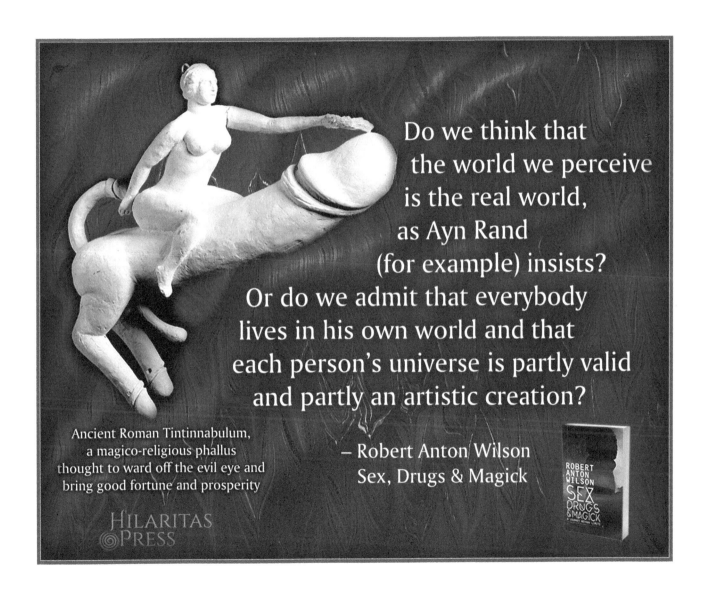

Do we think that
the world we perceive
is the real world,
as Ayn Rand
(for example) insists?
Or do we admit that everybody
lives in his own world and that
each person's universe is partly valid
and partly an artistic creation?

Ancient Roman Tintinnabulum,
a magico-religious phallus
thought to ward off the evil eye and
bring good fortune and prosperity

– Robert Anton Wilson
Sex, Drugs & Magick

HILARITAS
PRESS

ROBERT
ANTON
WILSON
SEX
DRUGS
& MAGICK

. . . it appears that most of what I have been calling Idolatry and Fundamentalism can be biologically described as normal primate behavior – mechanical imprinting and conditioning combined with normal territorial pugnacity.

– The New Inquisition

FNORD
BAPTIST
CHURCH

SUNDAY SERVICES
WORSHIP
9:00 AM
10:30 AM
BIBLE STUDY
9:00 AM
10:30 AM

JESUS IS FNORD
FULGUROUS EXHALATION
CONGLOBED IN A CLOUD
BY THE
CIRCUMFUSED HUMOUR

Tallius, writing in 1649, explained such anomalies, which have been seen, or hallucinated, to fall from the sky since the dawn of time, as the result of "fulgurous exhalation conglobed in a cloud by the circumfused humour."

While I don't totally buy that theory, since I don't understand it, it makes a little more sense than the segregating whirlwind of fundamentalism.

= Robert Anton Wilson
The New Inquisition

rawilson.com

149

The function of law and theology are the same: to keep the poor from taking back by violence what the rich have stolen by cunning.

— *The Historical Illuminatus Chronicles, Volume 3: Nature's God*

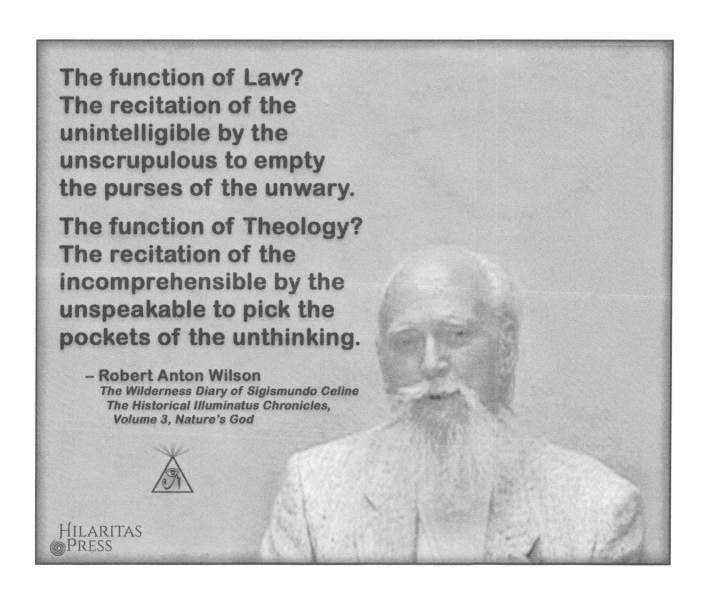

The function of Law?
The recitation of the
unintelligible by the
unscrupulous to empty
the purses of the unwary.

The function of Theology?
The recitation of the
incomprehensible by the
unspeakable to pick the
pockets of the unthinking.

– Robert Anton Wilson
The Wilderness Diary of Sigismundo Celine
The Historical Illuminatus Chronicles,
Volume 3, Nature's God

Some readers send me letters indicating that they have been extremely terrified; they have what William James called *negative conversion experiences*. On the other hand, other readers find it all hilarious and liberating. I got a letter from an ex-Moonie who said after he quit the Unification Church – which is a very totalitarian organization – after he quit, he was paranoid. He said for weeks he was sure they were going to come and get him, that he couldn't escape them, and that they would drag him back and force him to submit again. He said after reading *Illuminatus!* he laughed so much that he got over his paranoia. And that really delighted me because that was the intent of the book, to get people over such fears. And yet, other people are so scared by it they can't laugh – they practically freak out. That's because in all of my books I use the technique which is also used by Frederick Forsyth in much more conventional novels. It amuses me that Forsyth and I are using the same technique. We invented it independently – the technique of mixing in so many real facts that the reader is genuinely confused as to how much of it is real. He or she will say, if they read the newspapers, "My God, a lot of this is true." And I like to get the reader into that state of wondering if this much is true, how much of the rest of it is true. That's what I mean by Guerrilla Ontology; it's getting people to think, giving them puzzles that force them to think.

– Coincidance: A Head Test

152

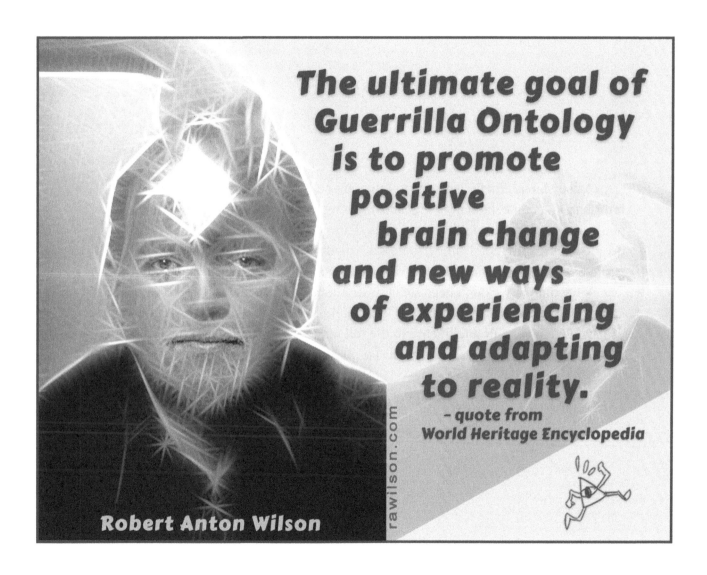

The ultimate goal of Guerrilla Ontology is to promote positive brain change and new ways of experiencing and adapting to reality.
– quote from World Heritage Encyclopedia

rawilson.com

Robert Anton Wilson

Censorship is chiefly intended to kill brain cells. When you don't get enough information, brain cells start dying, and anything that comes between the brain and potential information is killing brain cells. This is necessary in a scarcity economy so people won't figure out that hey, there's a crowd over there who are eating all the food while we're starving. The best thing is to keep people stupid, but since we're past that stage of evolution we don't need social institutions designed only to keep the people stupid, we can allow them to develop their intelligence to the full now. As a matter of fact, developing our intelligence to the full may now not only be "allowed," but it probably will prove to be a vast benefit for all of us.

– Email to the Universe:
and other alterations of consciousness

The Wall of Separation between
Church and State, like many other pious
pronouncements in our Constitution,
does not correspond with the way our
government actually functions.
In short, the Seven Forbidden Words
remain forbidden because pronouncing
them aloud might agitate some Stone
Age deity or other, and we still live in
the same web of Taboo that controls
other primitive peoples on this
boondocks planet.

– Robert Anton Wilson
Quantum Psychology

 HILARITAS PRESS

In *Cosmic Trigger II: Down to Earth,* you may remember, we touched briefly on the career of John Cleeves Symmes, soldier, hero, philosopher — the man who convinced a lot of people, in the early 19th Century, that the Earth has the shape of a balloon, i.e., a skin with nothing inside. President John Quincy Adams even, somewhat grudgingly, joined Congress in helping to fund an expedition to the South Pole to find the hole that Symmes claimed must exist there, according to his calculations.

The expedition never got to the Pole — skepticism ran high and funding ran low — and, as geology advanced, the hollow Earth theory suffered. Educated people knew too many facts that just did not fit any model but the rock-solid Earth that we all learn in school. The Experts all say so.

The hollow Earth theory never died, however. In 1871, a chap named Lyon, who claimed a professorship, and an associate named Sherman, who claimed an M.D. (both credentials seem dubious) brought forth The Hollow Globe, which not only argued the hollowness of our planet again but bluntly challenged the 2000-year-old Occidental habit of thinking of the only possible theological alternatives as Monotheism (One God) and Atheism (No God.) Lyon and Sherman proclaimed that many gods or spirits have collaboratively created the Cosmos.

– Cosmic Trigger III: My Life After Death

William James, father of American psychology, tells of meeting an old lady who told him the Earth rested on the back of a huge turtle.

"But, my dear lady,"
Professor James asked,
as politely as possible,
"what holds up the turtle?"

"Ah," she said, "that's easy.
He is standing on the back
of another turtle."

"Oh, I see," said Professor James,
still being polite.
"But would you be so good as to tell me
what holds up the second turtle?"

"It's no use, Professor," said the old lady,
realizing he was trying to lead her into
a logical trap.
"It's turtles-turtles-turtles, all the way!"

Robert Anton Wilson
Prometheus Rising

I am not so modest myself, as the reader may have noticed. I take full responsibility for the reality-labyrinths presented in my novels, and in alleged works of non-fiction like this catalog of blasphemy and heresy. My business is intellectual comedy, or surrealism, and is offered as entertainment for those bold, bad folks who are not frightened out of their wits by such guerilla ontology. Since I am the artist who invented this emic reality, I cannot regard it as anything else but an extension of my hilarious good humor – or my madness – as you will –

The people who believe the stuff that gets into my books seem as amusing to me as the people who are terrified or thrown into fury by them. I am not asking anybody to believe anything. I am asking only that you play a neurosemantic game with me, and observe what sort of reports you can consider with humor or dispassion and what sort of reports trigger terror or rage. If this be subversion, then so are the Marx Brothers and Monty Python.

– *The New Inquisition*

REALITY-LABYRINTH: existence regarded as a multiple-choice intelligence test; the sum total of reality-tunnels available to an open-minded or non-Fundamentalistic human at a given time and place.

— Robert Anton Wilson
The New Inquisition

HILARITAS PRESS

Phenomenologists and ethnomethodologists sometimes acknowledge an *etic reality* which is like unto the old- fashioned "objective reality" of traditional (pre-existentialist) philosophy and the ancient superstitions which have by now become "common sense". However, they point out that we cannot say anything meaningful about *etic* reality, because anything we can say has the structure of our *emic* reality — our social game rules (especially our language game) — built into it.

If you wish to deny this, please send me a complete description of etic reality, without using words, mathematics, music or other forms of human symbolism. (Send it express. I have wanted to see it for decades.)

Quantum Psychology: How Brain Software
Programs You and Your World

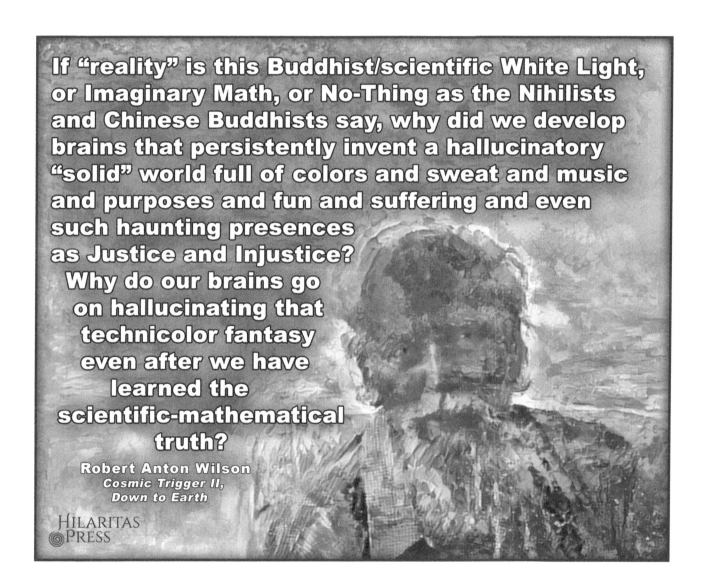

If "reality" is this Buddhist/scientific White Light, or Imaginary Math, or No-Thing as the Nihilists and Chinese Buddhists say, why did we develop brains that persistently invent a hallucinatory "solid" world full of colors and sweat and music and purposes and fun and suffering and even such haunting presences as Justice and Injustice? Why do our brains go on hallucinating that technicolor fantasy even after we have learned the scientific-mathematical truth?

Robert Anton Wilson
*Cosmic Trigger II,
Down to Earth*

HILARITAS
PRESS

163

I call this book Quantum Psychology rather than Quantum Philosophy because *understanding and internalizing (learning to use) these principles can decrease dogma, intolerance, compulsive behavior, hostility, etc. and also may increase openness, continuous learning, "growth" and empathy* — sombunall of which represent goals sought in most forms of psychotherapy, and sombunall forms of mystic religion.

– Quantum Psychology: How Brain Software
Programs You and Your World

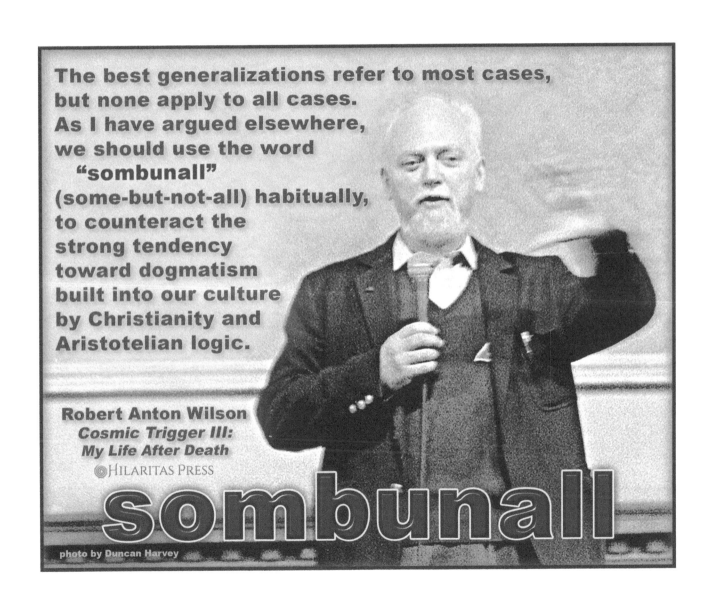

The best generalizations refer to most cases, but none apply to all cases. As I have argued elsewhere, we should use the word "sombunall" (some-but-not-all) habitually, to counteract the strong tendency toward dogmatism built into our culture by Christianity and Aristotelian logic.

Robert Anton Wilson
*Cosmic Trigger III:
My Life After Death*
HILARITAS PRESS

sombunall

photo by Duncan Harvey

How many times... have you encountered the saying, 'When the student is ready, the Master speaks?' Do you know why that is true? The door opens inward. The Master is everywhere, but the student has to open his mind to hear the Masters Voice.

– Masks of the Illuminati

"There's some truth somewhere in all this religious crap.
I gotta figure out where the true part of it is and disentangle it
from all the rest. (short pause) I'm still working on that project."
– Robert Anton Wilson

In 1967, after being fired from Harvard University for having weird ideas (but before being imprisoned), Dr. Timothy Leary, America's most controversial psychologist, published a pamphlet called "Start Your Own Religion," urging that every home should be a shrine, every man a priest, every woman a priestess. America, at that time, was ready for such an idea.

— *Coincidance: A Head Test*

The Javacrucians, a group
which looks suspiciously like a
parody of the Rosicrucians, has
selected the less-controversial
caffeine as its sacrament. It also
has the simplest theology in
history, teaching that one thing
only is necessary for salvation,
the American Coffee Ceremony
—a variation on the Japanese Tea
Ceremony. This is performed at
dawn, and you must face east,
towards the rising sun, as you
raise the cup to your lips.
When you take the first sip, you
must cry out with intense fervour,
"GOD, I needed that!"
If this is performed religiously
every morning, Javacrucians say,
you will face all life's challenges
   with a clear mind
      and a tranquil spirit.

      Robert Anton Wilson
      Coincidance: A Head Test

⦿ HILARITAS PRESS

169

Self-evaluation is very tricky. It's easy to go into either depression or megalomania. Instead of thinking how much have I accomplished, I prefer to think about what I can do this week to be a little less dumb than I was last week.

– Natural Law, Or Don't Put A Rubber On Your Willy
And Other Writings From A Natural Outlaw

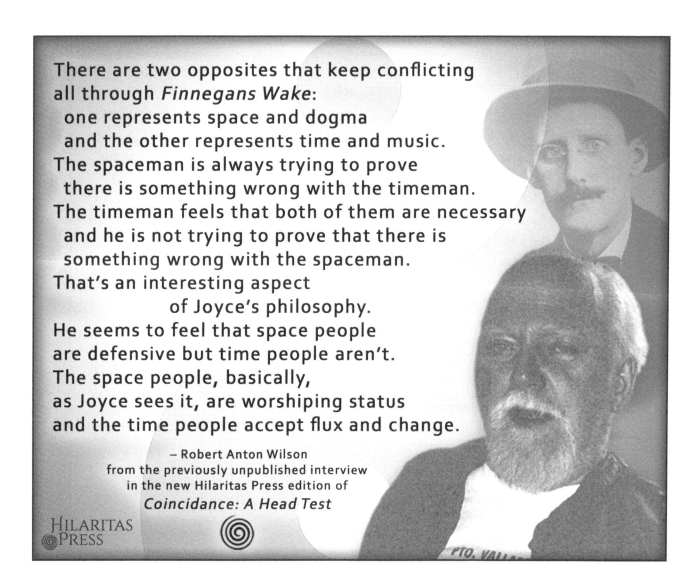

There are two opposites that keep conflicting
all through *Finnegans Wake*:
 one represents space and dogma
 and the other represents time and music.
The spaceman is always trying to prove
 there is something wrong with the timeman.
The timeman feels that both of them are necessary
 and he is not trying to prove that there is
 something wrong with the spaceman.
That's an interesting aspect
                    of Joyce's philosophy.
He seems to feel that space people
are defensive but time people aren't.
The space people, basically,
as Joyce sees it, are worshiping status
and the time people accept flux and change.

– Robert Anton Wilson
from the previously unpublished interview
in the new Hilaritas Press edition of
Coincidance: A Head Test

HILARITAS
PRESS

Among my sins, I turned Shea on to Weed. I turned a lot of people on to Weed in those days. I had a Missionary Zeal about it, but now that I think back, so did a lot of others at *Playboy* in those days. Maybe I should say that I helped turn Bob on to the Herb.

On one gloriously idiotic occasion we got our hands on some super pot from Thailand and had the dumbest conversation of our lives.

"What did you say?" Shea would ask, concentrating intensely, like somebody enquiring of Socrates about the meaning of justice . . .

I'd grapple with that abysmal enigma, but amid millions of new sensations and a rush of Cosmic Insights, I'd lose the question before I could find an answer to it. "What . . . did . . . you . . . say?" I would ask slowly, trying to deal with the problem reasonably.

"I asked . . . uh . . ." He paused to reconsider the gravity of the problem. "Um what did you ah just ask?"

And so on, for what seemed like Hindu yugas or maybe even kalpas. That night inspired the "Islands of Micro-Amnesia" in *Illuminatus!* Maybe a similar night inspired the Lotus Eaters in the Odyssey?

– Cosmic Trigger III: My Life After Death

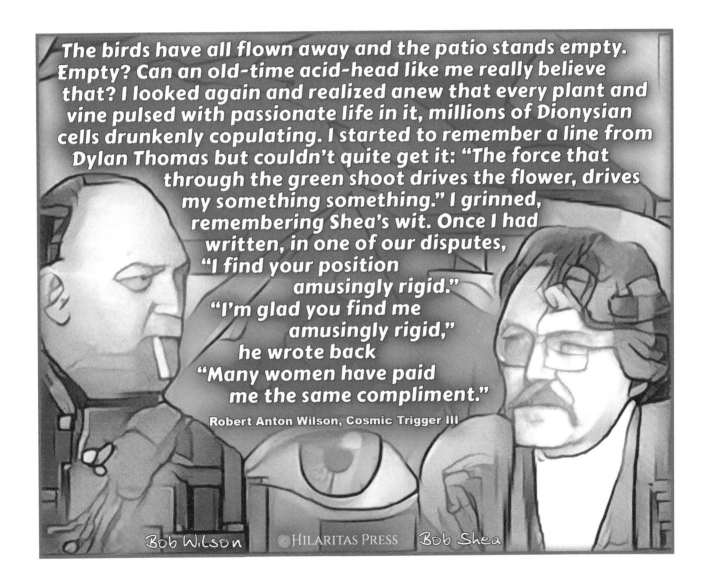

In his final blog on January 6, Wilson wrote: "I don't see how to take death seriously. I look forward without dogmatic optimism, but without dread. I love you all and I deeply implore you to keep the lasagna flying." Actually, it was expected that he would die seven months earlier. On June 19, 2006, he sent this haiku (with one syllable missing) to his electronic cabal:

Well what do you know?
Another day has passed
and I'm still not not.

— from Paul Krassner's afterword for Email to the Universe, and other alterations of consciousness

By the way, I have always felt that Crowley's "Do What Thou Wilt" is good . . . The question then becomes "What do we will to do." Most of the Crowleyites I've met (yourself excluded) seem to have decided they will make pompous asses of themselves. Which is fine with me. But I'm delighted that we've found the three obvious steps that a reasonably educated God takes: SMI²LE.

– Timothy Leary quoted in Cosmic Trigger I: Final Secret of the Illuminati

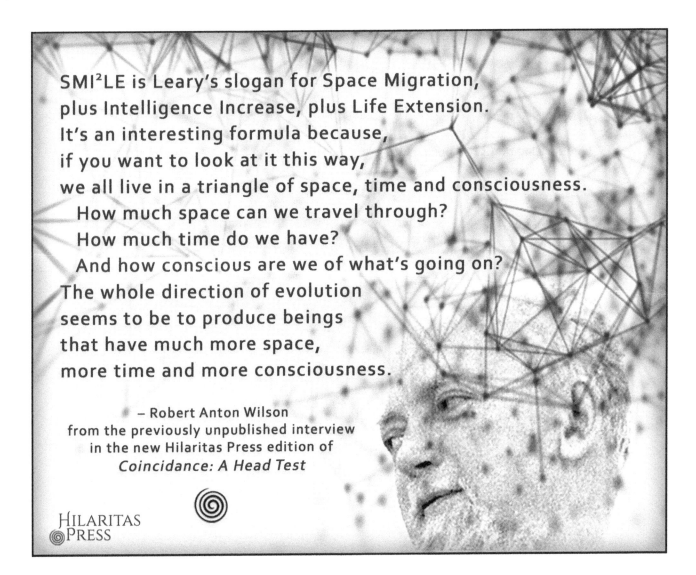

SMI²LE is Leary's slogan for Space Migration,
plus Intelligence Increase, plus Life Extension.
It's an interesting formula because,
if you want to look at it this way,
we all live in a triangle of space, time and consciousness.
   How much space can we travel through?
   How much time do we have?
   And how conscious are we of what's going on?
The whole direction of evolution
seems to be to produce beings
that have much more space,
more time and more consciousness.

– Robert Anton Wilson
from the previously unpublished interview
in the new Hilaritas Press edition of
Coincidance: A Head Test

HILARITAS
PRESS

Claude Shannon's famous equation for the information content of a message, H, reads

$$H = -\Sigma p_i \log_e p_i$$

The reader terrorized by mathematics (persuaded by incompetent teachers that "I can't understand that stuff") need not panic. Σ merely means "the sum of." The symbol, P_i, tells us what we will summarize, namely the various probabilities (p_1, p_2 . . . etc. to p_n, where n equals the number of signals in the message) that we can *predict in advance* what will come next. The logarithmic function merely shows that this relationship does not accumulate additively but logarithmically. *Notice the minus sign*. The information in a message equals the negative of the probabilities that you can predict what will come next every step of the way. The easier you can predict a message, the less information the message contains.

Quantum Psychology: How Brain Software
Programs You and Your World

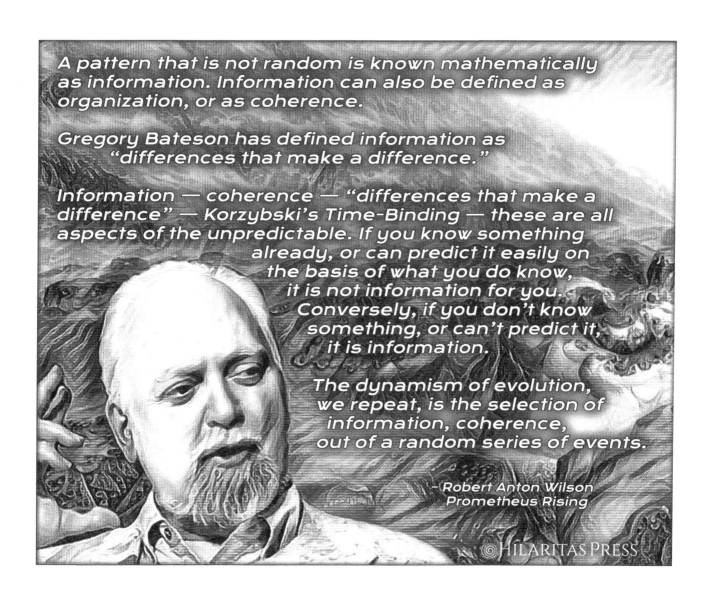

A pattern that is not random is known mathematically as information. Information can also be defined as organization, or as coherence.

Gregory Bateson has defined information as "differences that make a difference."

Information — coherence — "differences that make a difference" — Korzybski's Time-Binding — these are all aspects of the unpredictable. If you know something already, or can predict it easily on the basis of what you do know, it is not information for you. Conversely, if you don't know something, or can't predict it, it is information.

The dynamism of evolution, we repeat, is the selection of information, coherence, out of a random series of events.

– Robert Anton Wilson
Prometheus Rising

© HILARITAS PRESS

179

If human stupidity in general decreased, there would be less opposition to original thinking and new approaches to our old problems, less censorship and less bigotry.

– Prometheus Rising

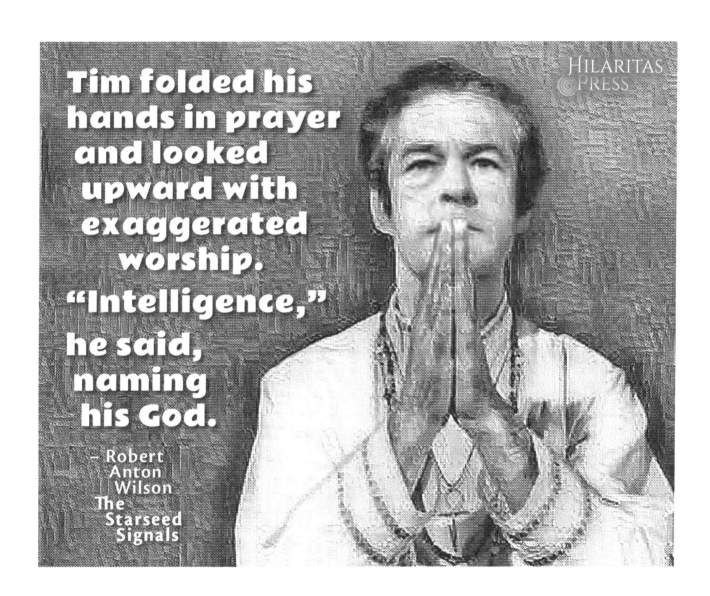

Tim folded his hands in prayer and looked upward with exaggerated worship. "Intelligence," he said, naming his God.

— Robert Anton Wilson
The Starseed Signals

HILARITAS PRESS

181

A sinister rumor, widely believed in the Occident, holds that after death we may go to a place called Heaven. From all the descriptions I've read, it sounds dreadful to me. It seems to have a population made up entirely of some gang of Christians; the experts on Heaven disagree about which conglomeration of Christians will qualify, but they always seem to think that they personally belong to that elite group. An eternity with people that conceited seems intolerable to me, but fortunately I am not a Christian so I won't be consigned to such a boring place.

An even more nefarious report appears in the United States Marine Corps hymn:

> If the Army and the Navy
> ever looked on Heaven's scenes
> they would find the streets were guarded
> by the United States Marines

A place where every street is guarded by Marines sounds like a particularly vicious police state, especially if Christians run it, and I definitely don't want to go there, even for a visit. I wouldn't even wish it on my worst enemy, if I had any enemies. (Some people hate me for the books I write, but I refuse to hate them back, so they don't count as enemies.)

Fortunately, as noted, I don't qualify for Heaven, with all its harps and fanatic Christians and martial law by Marines.

– Email to the Universe,
and other alterations of consciousness

A bored angel waits at the threshold of the Gates of Eternity. A confused looking man in pyjamas makes his way through the audience and stands before the angel.

ANGEL
Go no further, O mortal, until you have proven to me your worthiness to enter paradise.

MAN
Just a minute, now. First of all, can you prove to me this is a real Heaven and not just the wishful fantasy of my disordered mind undergoing death?

The Angel is lost for words.

VOICE FROM BEHIND CURTAIN
Let him in – he's one of us!

HILARITAS
PRESS

183

When I got to the steps of the Five Sided Castle somebody was passing around a joint. I took a toke, and thought I would someday tell my grandchildren that I smoked Weed on the steps of the Pentagon.

Cosmic Trigger II: Down to Earth

"They cling to their joints and Model Agnosticism."
– Olga Struthio

"We are all giants, raised by pygmies, who have learned to walk with a perpetual mental crouch. Unleashing our full stature – our total brain power – is what this book is all about."

We are all giants, raised by pygmies, who have learned to walk with a perpetual mental crouch. Unleashing our full stature – our total brain power – is what this book is all about.
– Prometheus Rising

My own books, especially *Prometheus Rising*, give numerous examples of how optimism (a "Winner Script" in the language of Transactional Analysis) can resolve psychological and social problems that seem incurable to those obsessed by pessimism (a "Loser Script" in T.A.).

Quantum Psychology: How Brain Software
Programs You and Your World

Damnation by Definition

These fragments come from a book I started in 1964 called Authority and Submission. *When five publishers in a row rejected it, I gave up attempting books for six full years and only wrote shorter pieces. I still had a lot of pessimism and masochism in those days.*

Parts of Authority and Submission *eventually got rewritten and incorporated into* Illuminatus! *and* Prometheus Rising.

The most thoroughly and relentlessly Damned, banned, excluded, condemned, forbidden, ostracized, ignored, suppressed, repressed, robbed, brutalized and defamed of all Damned Things is the individual human being . . .

– Email to the Universe:
and other alterations of consciousness

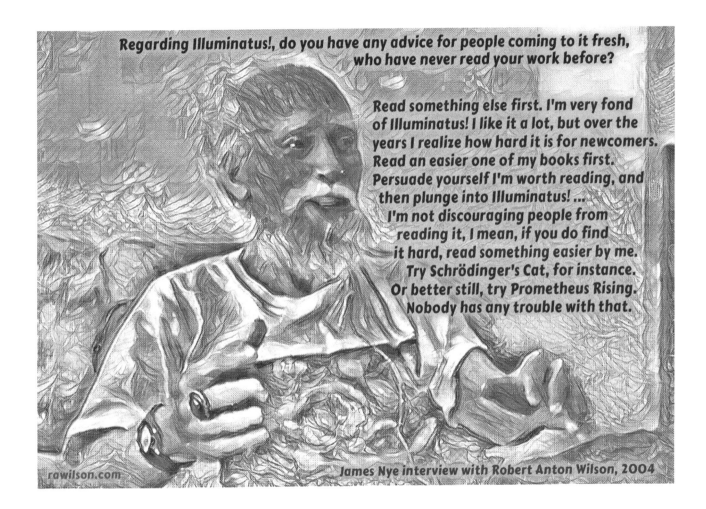

Regarding Illuminatus!, do you have any advice for people coming to it fresh, who have never read your work before?

Read something else first. I'm very fond of Illuminatus! I like it a lot, but over the years I realize how hard it is for newcomers. Read an easier one of my books first. Persuade yourself I'm worth reading, and then plunge into Illuminatus! ... I'm not discouraging people from reading it, I mean, if you do find it hard, read something easier by me. Try Schrödinger's Cat, for instance. Or better still, try Prometheus Rising. Nobody has any trouble with that.

rawilson.com

James Nye interview with Robert Anton Wilson, 2004

OM was originally instigated by Ho Chih Zen, of the Frisian Liberation Front, who is the same person but not the same individual as Lord Omar Khayyam Ravenhurst, author of *The Honest Book of Truth*. The guiding philosophy is that originally proposed in *The Theory of Games and Economic Behavior* by von Neumann and Morgenstern: namely, that the only strategy which an opponent cannot predict is a random strategy. The foundation had already been laid by the late Malaclypse the Younger, K.S.C., when he proclaimed, "We Discordians must stick apart." This radical decentralization of all Discordian enterprises created a built-in random factor even before Operation Mind-fuck was proposed. To this day, neither Ho Chih Zen himself nor any other Discordian apostle knows for sure who is or is not involved in any phase of Operation Mindfuck or what activities they are or are not engaged in as part of that project. Thus, the outsider is immediately trapped in a double-bind: the only safe assumption is that anything a Discordian does is somehow related to OM, but, since this leads directly to paranoia, this is not a "safe" assumption after all, and the "risky" hypothesis that whatever the Discordians are doing is harmless may be "safer" in the long run, perhaps. *Every aspect of OM follows, or accentuates, this double-bind.*

OM projects vary from the trivial to the colossal . . .

– Illuminatus!

Thoughtful Discordians have realized Operation Mindfuck worked a little too well and rather than just Operation Mindfixing it, they feel a need to outsmart the little realityfuckers who were a little too mindfucked, and so they want to turn OM into Operation Mindfox.

"Reality is what you can get away with." — Robert Anton Wilson

rawilson.com

Actually, I no longer disbelieve in the Illuminati, but I don't believe in them yet, either. Let us explain that odd remark quickly, before we go any further in the murk. In researching occult conspiracies, one eventually faces a crossroad of mythic proportions (called Chapel Perilous in the trade). You come out the other side either a stone paranoid or an agnostic; there is no third way. I came out an agnostic.

Chapel Perilous, like the mysterious entity called "I," cannot be located in the space-time continuum; it is weightless, odorless, tasteless and undetectable by ordinary instruments. Indeed, like the Ego, it is even possible to deny that it is there. And yet, even more like the Ego, once you are inside it, there doesn't seem to be any way to ever get out again, until you suddenly discover that it has been brought into existence by thought and does not exist outside thought. *Every thing you fear* is waiting with slavering jaws in Chapel Perilous, but if you are armed with the wand of intuition, the cup of sympathy, the sword of reason and the pentacle of valor, you will find there (the legends say) the Medicine of Metals, the Elixir of Life, the Philosopher's Stone, True Wisdom and Perfect Happiness.

– Cosmic Trigger I: Final Secret of the Illuminati

Marijuana, of course, also puts you on the fifth circuit – right-brain rapture – but only temporarily. It was one of Crowley's secret teachings, only passed on verbally to promising students, that the combination marijuana + tantra was the key to rapid mutation into a permanent Rapture Circuit.

– Cosmic Trigger I: Final Secret of the Illuminati

The first pot-smoker I ever knew was a black jazz musician who was my friend in the late 1950s. Although unwilling to experiment with "drugs" at that point, I was curious enough to ask about the experience. One of his illustrations has always stuck in my mind. "Take a quarter out of your pocket," he said. "Look at it. You don't really see it . A little kid handling a quarter for the first time really sees it. Now, if you smoke a reefer and then look at the quarter, you'll really see it again, for the first time since childhood." This is what Leary called level 4, sensory consciousness. (It is renamed circuit 5, the neurosomatic or rapture circuit, in his current writings.)

– Robert Anton Wilson
The Starseed Signals

HILARITAS PRESS

Dr. Bohm's third alternative, modification of our ideas of space and time, could lead us anywhere . . . including back to the Berkeleyan/Kantian notion that space and time do not exist, except as human projections, like persistent optical illusions. (Some think Relativity already demonstrates that . . . and some will recall Mr. Yeats again, and that Kerry farmer . . .) All particles remain correlated because they never move in space or time, because space and time only exist "in our heads."

– *Email to the Universe:*
and other alterations of consciousness

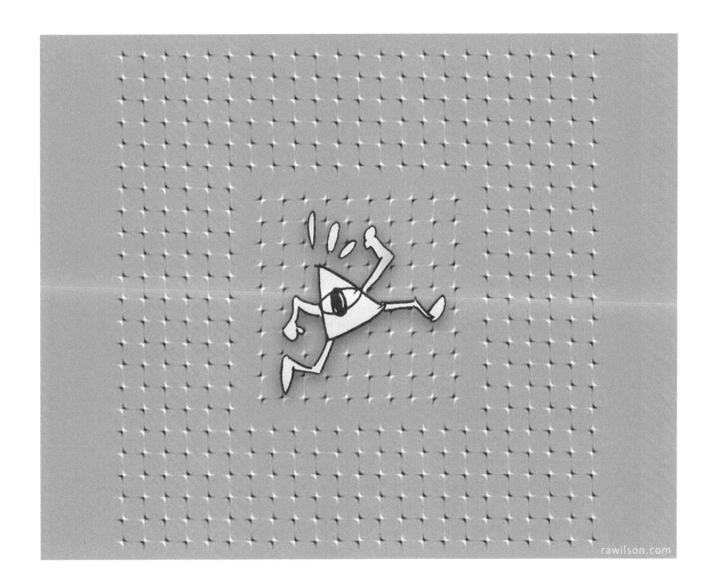

197

In pre-ethological terms, the emotional-territorial circuit is what we usually call "ego." *Ego is simply the mammalian recognition of one's status in the pack;* it is a "role" as sociologists say, a single brain circuit which mistakes itself for the whole Self, the entire brain-mind apparatus. The "egotist" behaves like "a two year old," in the common saying, because Ego is the imprint of the toddling and toilet-training stage.

– Prometheus Rising

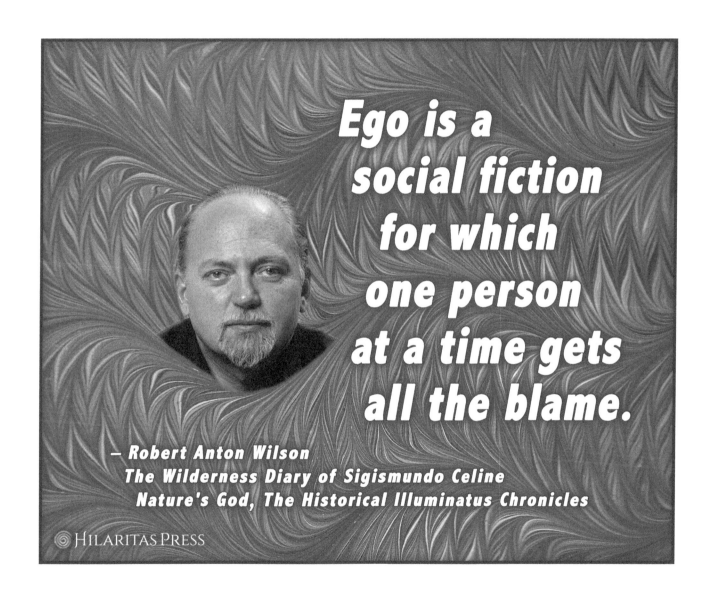

Ego is a social fiction for which one person at a time gets all the blame.

— Robert Anton Wilson
The Wilderness Diary of Sigismundo Celine
Nature's God, The Historical Illuminatus Chronicles

HILARITAS PRESS

I'm not sure if I want to become Immortal. I'm not sure that any "I" can. But I am damned sure that I can live many thousands of years, more or less as "me," and that it will be most interesting, and that maybe some sort of "I" can graduate to a Immortality.

Immortality will necessarily involve Neurologic, i.e. serial reincarnation in the "same" body (more or less). Much metaphysical mystery about ego and memory and identity after re-imprinting becomes more efficient.

– Letter from Robert Anton Wilson to Greg Hill in
The Starseed Signals

rawilson.com

201

De Sade in his marvelously frank way analyzed the joy in frightening people as a refined form of the sadistic compulsions that drove him, and many psychoanalysts have noted the same connection. Sermons on hell, to hysterical and fainting congregations, are the psychological equivalent of the racks, whips, iron boots and other overtly sadistic implements of the Holy Inquisition.

– Coincidance: A Heat Test

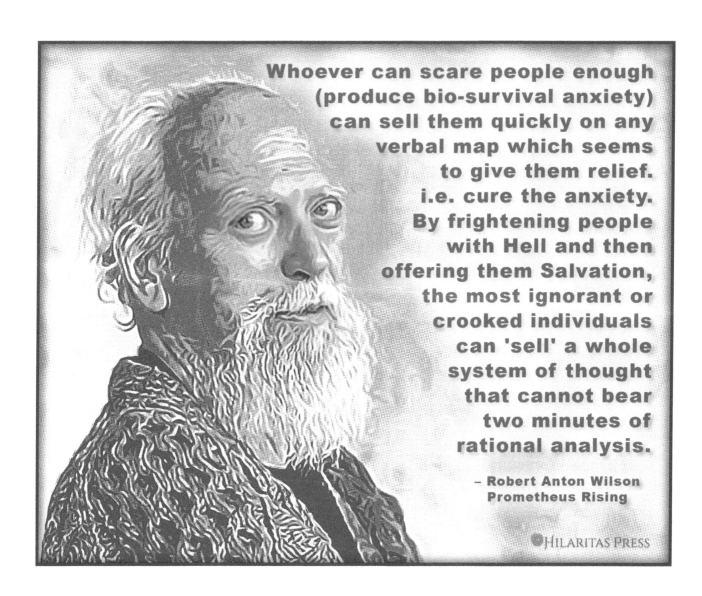

Whoever can scare people enough
(produce bio-survival anxiety)
can sell them quickly on any
verbal map which seems
to give them relief.
i.e. cure the anxiety.
By frightening people
with Hell and then
offering them Salvation,
the most ignorant or
crooked individuals
can 'sell' a whole
system of thought
that cannot bear
two minutes of
rational analysis.

– Robert Anton Wilson
Prometheus Rising

HILARITAS PRESS

The metaprogramming circuit is *not* a trap. As Joyce would say, it only looks as like it as damn it. Simply accept that the universe is so structured that it can see itself, and that this self-reflexive arc is built into our frontal lobes, so that consciousness contains an infinite regress, and all we can do is make models of ourselves making models . . .

Well, at that point, the only thing to do is relax and enjoy the show.

This is what the Hindus call *Shiva-darshana*, or the divine dance. You are still in life, or life is in you, but since there are infinite aspects to everything, especially to the "you" who is observing/creating all these muddles and models, *there are no limits*.

The only sensible goal, then, is to try to build a reality-tunnel for next week that is bigger, funnier, sexier, more optimistic and generally less boring than any previous reality-tunnel.

– Prometheus Rising

It is a great moment when the hoodwink is removed, and the most famous Rationalist of the age sees that he has been engaged in revolutionary rituals with the most famous Scientist of the age – the man who hurled lightning bolts at the Vatican faces the man who tamed the lightning with a key on a kite string.

After the initiation, some say, M. Voltaire and M. Franklin had a banquet with the Marquis de Condorcet and discussed science and philosophy. The big gorilla was trying to make it work . . .

. . . M. Condorcet then grew more enthusiastic (they were on their third bottle of wine by then) and announced that he could foresee major reforms in the next century alone. M. Franklin listened, spellbound, as M. Condorcet pictured for them endless caves and labyrinths—a world in which education was free for all, boys and girls alike, and schools were taught by rational well-educated men and women, not by narrow-minded priests and nuns. A world in which insurance companies, some run by private investors and some by the state, would pay decent premiums to those injured and disabled, and even to those unemployed, by economic recession. A world in which the state would loan the money for scientific and technological research not even imaginable today, perhaps even to fly to the moon. A world in which every city had free public libraries, like the one M. Franklin had started in Philadelphia, and the state and private investors would offer "illness insurance" so nobody would die for lack of money to pay the doctors. M. Franklin agreed that all of this might happen in a century, but some of it would probably take two centuries.

– Coincidance: A Head Test

America has more ignorant people than any other industrial nation, because of certain differences between European and American capitalists. . . . Europeans believe they can make bigger profits with very well educated workers . . . Americans believe they can make bigger profits with an ignorant and docile working class.

Robert Anton Wilson
Reality Is What You Can Get Away With

©Hilaritas Press

207

An interesting Mexican ritual involving marijuana is described in Peter Furst's *Flesh of the Gods*, concerning the Tepe-hua Indians. They regard the plant as potentially dangerous (just like our solons in Washington) but control it by ritual rather than by law, dedicating it to the worship of the three most powerful local gods, Jesus, the Virgin Mary, and the sun. Praying, sometimes laughing, they get high amid song, speeches, ringing of bells, dancing, chanting and whistling. The ceremony not only allows each worshipper to confront his god directly, but is believed to cure any illnesses the children of the village might have.

– Sex, Drugs & Magick: A Journey Beyond Limits

THEY DON'T WANT ANYBODY TO GET HIGH, BECAUSE PEOPLE WHO GET HIGH GET HAPPY, AND PEOPLE WHO GET HAPPY GET AMBITIOUS, UPPITY AND RAMBUNCTIOUS, AND THEY WANT EVERYBODY TO BE DEPRESSED. BUT THE HIGH IS PART OF THE CURE.

ROBERT ANTON WILSON
MAYBE LOGIC
DOCUMENTARY

RAWILSON.COM

In India, recreational use of cannabis seems to go back to around 500 BC and one myth claims it was given to mankind by Shiva, god of sex, intoxication and mysticism; in other versions of this legend, Shiva is actually incarnate in the Indian hemp plant. From about that time to the present, Indian doctors have prescribed cannabis extracts for dysentery, sunstroke, indigestion, lack of appetite and other conditions. Shivites use it in their religious worship, and other sects believe it is useful as spiritual preparation for reading holy writings or entering sacred places.

– Sex, Drugs & Magick: A Journey Beyond Limits

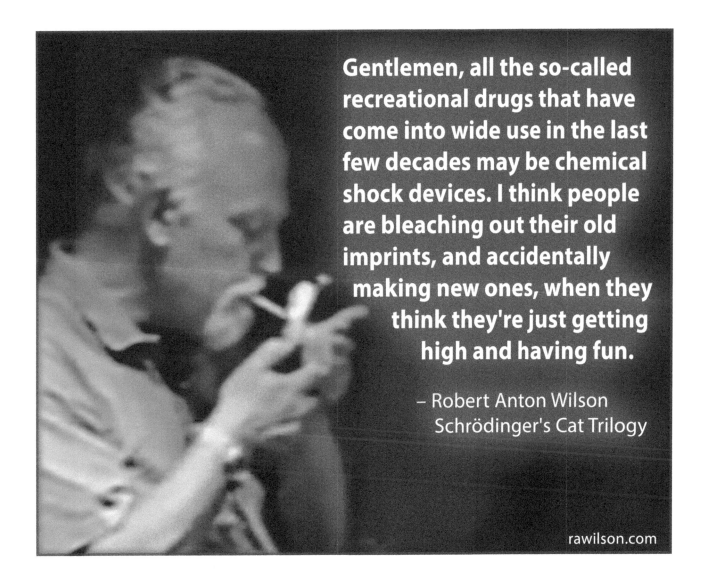

Gentlemen, all the so-called recreational drugs that have come into wide use in the last few decades may be chemical shock devices. I think people are bleaching out their old imprints, and accidentally making new ones, when they think they're just getting high and having fun.

– Robert Anton Wilson
Schrödinger's Cat Trilogy

rawilson.com

I am sourly amused that some critics complain that I am "too optimistic" or "too Utopian." I guess critics of that ilk only read every second page. My "optimism" is an act of will – a revolutionary act of defiance, perhaps – but it is not based on any innocent illusions about what human beings have been doing to each other since the dawn of history.

– Coincidance: A Head Test

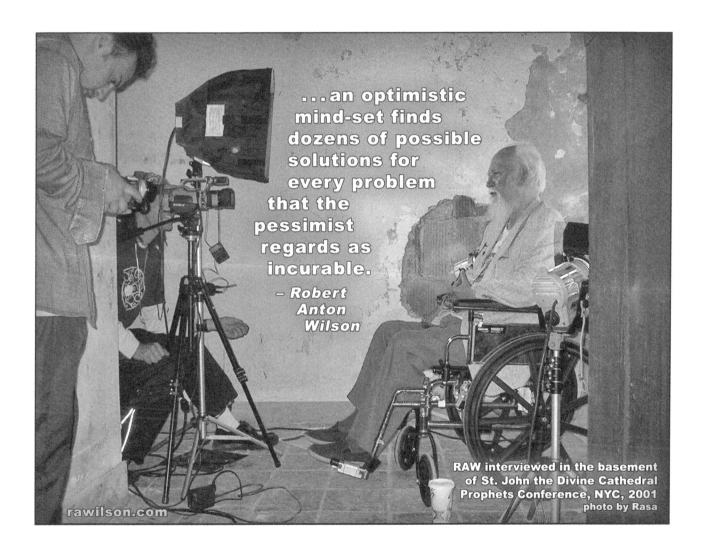

...an optimistic mind-set finds dozens of possible solutions for every problem that the pessimist regards as incurable.

– Robert Anton Wilson

RAW interviewed in the basement of St. John the Divine Cathedral Prophets Conference, NYC, 2001
photo by Rasa

rawilson.com

213

Narrator: The New Age is the greatest evolutionary breakthrough since our ancestors crawled out of the sea onto the land. It is a biological, technological, neurological, and psychological transformation unprecedented in history.

Midget: Wait a goddamn minute here. You just said it was a load of bullshit.

Narrator: That's right.

Midget: Well, which is it?

Narrator: It's both. Some things called New Age are tremendous evolutionary mutations. Other things called New Age are pure bullshit.

Midget: Well, how can we tell the difference?

Narrator: The only way to distinguish the pure gold from the counterfeit is . . . to learn to think for yourself. *To learn to think for yourself.* Got it? To stop being robots.

– Reality Is What You Can Get Away With

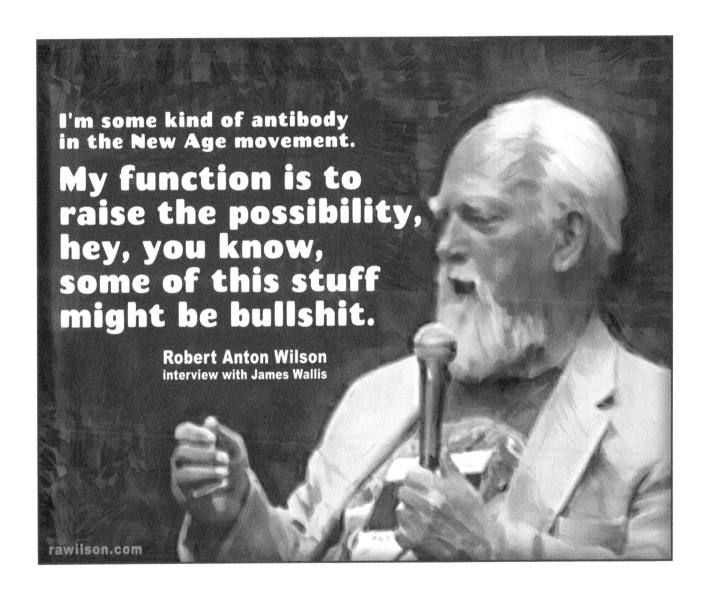

I'm some kind of antibody in the New Age movement. My function is to raise the possibility, hey, you know, some of this stuff might be bullshit.

Robert Anton Wilson
interview with James Wallis

rawilson.com

215

A disciple is an asshole looking for a human being to attach itself to!

– Reality Is What You Can Get Away With

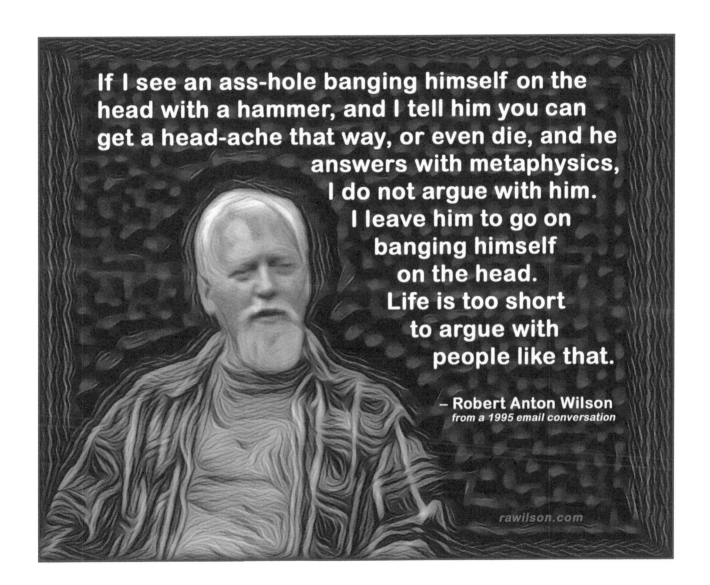

If I see an ass-hole banging himself on the head with a hammer, and I tell him you can get a head-ache that way, or even die, and he answers with metaphysics, I do not argue with him. I leave him to go on banging himself on the head. Life is too short to argue with people like that.

— Robert Anton Wilson
from a 1995 email conversation

rawilson.com

I kept thinking about it on my way to the office. If I pointed out a fnord to somebody who hadn't been de-conditioned, as Hagbard deconditioned me, what would he or she say? They'd probably read the word before or after it. "No this word," I'd say. And they would again read an adjacent word. But would their panic level rise as the threat came closer to consciousness? I preferred not to try the experiment; it might have ended with a psychotic fugue in the subject. The conditioning, after all, went back to grade school. No wonder we all hate those teachers so much: we have a dim, masked memory of what they've done to us in converting us into good and faithful servants for the Illuminati.

– *Illuminatus!*

Instant FNORD
JUST ADD ORDER!

Recommended by
22 out of 23
Professional Fnordticians!

219

Q: How much credence do you lend to the idea that genuine aliens could be involved in some of these conspiracies in real-world-terms? Do aliens exist for you, and do you think they conspire with the government?

A: I think the literal form of that model, brought forth by Bill Cooper and William Moore and others of that persuasion, is a wonderful metaphor, a great plot for a science-fiction story. But I can't take it literally. I just can't believe in it. The aliens in these scenarios come right out of bad 1950's science-fiction B-movies. I'd find it easier to believe that Snow White and the Seven Dwarfs were piloting all the UFOs . . . or the Three Stooges . . .

On the other hand, the idea that there are forces we don't understand involved in some of the shenanigans on this planet does have a certain plausibility to it. The more you look into these things, the more you feel that there is a player on the other side. I feel like Thomas Henry Huxley, the great agnostic – a guy who was an enemy of religion all his life – and yet in one passage in one of his essays, he says we're like people playing a chess game, where the pieces are the phenomena of the universe, the rules of the game are the laws of nature we've discovered so far, but the player on the other side is still invisible. I classify UFOs, and the paranormal in general, and Fortean phenomena as acts of the "player" on the other side that we don't understand yet.

– Email to the Universe:
and other alterations of consciousness

. . . we all need Olga . . . Without her, we might take ourselves – and featherless biped politics in general – too damned seriously, following the usual "slippery slope" downward from Ideology to Idiocy. We need the perspectives of our feathered cousins, no matter how weird they may sound at times.

– Email to the Universe:
and other alterations of consciousness

223

It can be safely said that human psychology would be entirely different – radically different – if tits had never appeared in evolution. We will give repeated examples of this as we proceed. For the time being, just consider the warmest kinds of love you have experienced with other humans, sexually or platonically, with women or with men who have been friends or helpers to you. Do you think we would have any of that sort of emotion without the conditioning received at the breast? Take a look at how iguanas or other reptiles (who are not suckled) relate to each other, and make a guess about how many of the "cold, snaky bastards" you've met were either bottle-fed or nursed by mothers who had negative feelings about nursing. Wilhelm Reich said that traumas received during nursing from mothers who are uptight about their mammalian functions are "the source of the human no" – the dawn of the feeling that there's something wrong with the universe and it has to be fixed as bloodily and quickly as possible.

– Ishtar Rising: Why the Goddess Went to Hell
and What to Expect Now That She's Returning

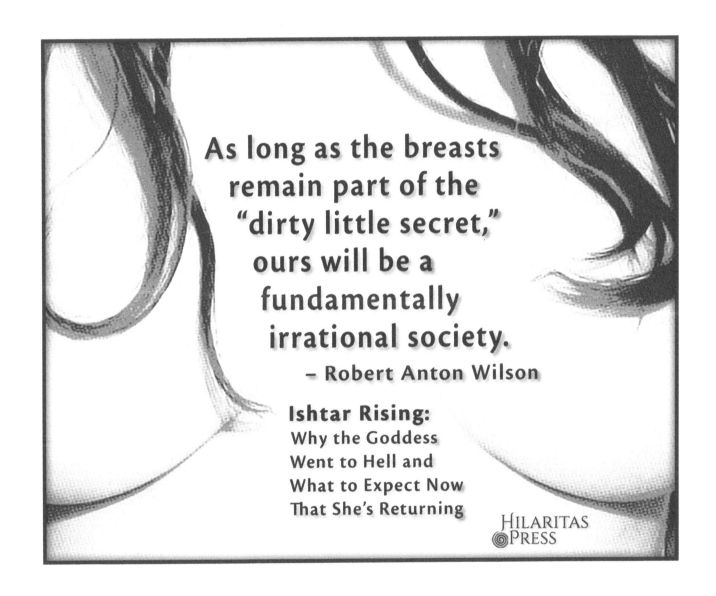

As long as the breasts
remain part of the
"dirty little secret,"
ours will be a
fundamentally
irrational society.

– Robert Anton Wilson

Ishtar Rising:
Why the Goddess
Went to Hell and
What to Expect Now
That She's Returning

HILARITAS
⊚PRESS

4. The Socio-Sexual System. At puberty, the DNA unleashes messenger RNA molecules which notify all subsystems that mating time has arrived. The body metamorphizes totally, and the nervous system ("mind") changes in the process. A new "self" appears.

As usual, imprinting and genetics play a major role, with conditioning and learning modifying but seldom radically altering genetic-imprinted imperatives. If the environment provides a sex-positive imprint, adult sexuality will have a joyous and even "transcendental" quality; if the environment provides a sex-negative imprint, sexuality will remain disturbed or problematical for life.

– Quantum Psychology: How Brain Software
Programs You and Your World

Considering the wide variety of philosophies available to any of us – nudism and Buddhism, scientific materialism and snake worship, Communism and vegetarianism, subjective Idealism and Existentialism, Methodism and Shinto, etc. – the fact that most people remain in the same reality-tunnel as their parents, does indicate that acculturalization is a mind control process. We are all giants, raised by pygmies, who have learned to walk with a perpetual mental crouch. Unleashing our full stature – our total brain power – is what this book is all about.

– Prometheus Rising

We are all giants,
raised by pygmies,
who have learned to walk
with a perpetual mental crouch.

Unleashing our full stature –
our total brain power –
is what this book is all about.

Robert Anton Wilson
Prometheus Rising

Leary now symbolizes intelligence-studying intelligence by the mark, I^2.

On the lower levels, you see with one "I," so to speak.

On the higher levels, you see with many "I"s.

And space-time shifts from three Euclidean dimensions to non-Euclidean multi-dimensionality.

– Cosmic Trigger I: Final Secret Of The Illuminati

I can only conclude that I am indeed like a visitor from non-Euclidean dimensions whose outlines are perplexing to the Euclidean inhabitants of various dogmatic Flatlands.

– Robert Anton Wilson, *Email to the Universe*

In 1974, I stopped publishing *The Realist* because I ran out of money and taboos. In 1985, I re-launched it in a newsletter format. For a feature story in the born-again *Realist*, I contacted Bob Wilson. There was a one-inch news item about a convention in Italy of the Married Roman Catholic Priests Association, representing 70,000 priests who had married in defiance of the Vatican. I gave the clipping to him.

"Bob, should you choose to accept this assignment, I'd like you to cover this event as though you had actually been there."

Wilson wrote his report, and even I almost believed that he had actually gone to the married priests convention. Next, there was a tiny news item about the first International Orgasm Conference, and I assigned him to cover that event too, as though he had actually been there. *The Realist* was back in apocryphal business. This time I published the final issue in 2001. But Robert Anton Wilson is still alive in the form of his literary legacy. May he rest in lasagna.

– from Paul Krassner's afterword for Email to the Universe,
and other alterations of consciousness

233

I liked old Yoshikami. His school of Buddhism was Shinran, a variation on Amida Buddhism, which in turn is based on faith in Amida, the Buddha of Boundless Compassion. Amida refused to accept Nirvana until every sentient being could enter that blessed quenched state along with him. Amida Buddhists believe that if you call on Amida just once *with true faith* – saying *"Namu Amida Butsu"* (Japanese for "In the name of Amida Buddha") – you will reach Nirvana eventually, even if you fuck up so much that it takes a couple of hundred thousand incarnations to get you there.

Amida never gives up on you. He's like a finance company that way – a reverse finance company that wants to give you Something for Nothing.

– Cosmic Trigger II: Down To Earth

Kindness remains,
to me,
the most
wonderful miracle
in this
incomprehensible
universe.

– Robert Anton Wilson
Cosmic Trigger III

235

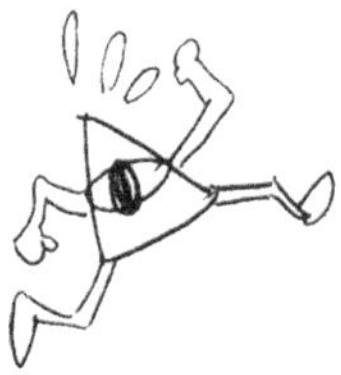

Bob & Rasa
January 2006
Capitola, California

Photographs of Bob and Rasa by Marlis Jermutus

Bob and Rasa

Richard Rasa, musician, writer, graphic artist, webmaster, publisher and close friend of Robert Anton Wilson, created over the years a series of memes for The Robert Anton Wilson Trust, rawilson.com, Hilaritas Press and Flying Lasagna Enterprises. Rasa's illustrations were first used by Wilson for his satirical Guns and Dope Party campaign and website, and in his book, *Email to the Universe*.

Rasa (it's his last name, but everyone calls him, "Rasa") was introduced to Robert Anton Wilson and his wife Arlen by his old friend, German abstract artist, Marlis Jermutus. Marlis, her husband Bastian, and Rasa (who together have a music group called Starseed) used to visit Bob and Arlen regularly in Santa Cruz, and later after Arlen passed, in Bob's apartment in Capitola, California. Rasa and Bob formed a strong friendship over hours of lively conversations. Rasa helped Bob set up his first email account, and they started sending nearly daily emails back and forth. When Bob figured out the "cc" protocol, he started to include other friends, and soon after, RAW's "Groupmind" email group was formed. We asked Rasa to offer some reflections . . .

I sent an email to Bob's new email address with a "welcome to the net" greeting, and as was the custom, I inserted some humor someone had passed on to me in an email. The humor was a list of about 90 why-did-the-chicken-cross-the-road jokes from the perspective of notable people, like: Plato, Karl Marx, Machiavelli, Timothy Leary, Douglas Adams, Carl Jung, John Paul Sartre, Buddha, Salvador Dali, Werner Heisenberg, Groucho Marx, etc. Both of us were amused that someone had included what we both thought was a rather lame joke of what "Robert Anton Wilson" would say about the chicken.

Robert Anton Wilson: Because agents of the Ancient Illuminated Roosters of Cooperia were controlling it with their Orbital Mind-Control Lasers as part of their master plan to take over the world's egg production.

Bob replied to that email with some additions to that list. He wrote,

Dear Rasa:

Thanks for the chicken jokes. A few more I thought of:

Thomas Jefferson: All hens are endowed by Nature and Nature's God with certain unalienable rights, and among these are life, liberty and the pursuit of the other side.

James Joyce: An ova eggspressed! Mrs. Hahn, Cock's wife, flapped up a stormin drang (one louve, one fear) and, like any tennis son, charged like a lewd brigade, clucking and clacking like a horsenfifer, nobirdy avair soar anywing like that load allmarshey.

Bart Simpson: I will not use the school chicken as a frisbee. I will not use the school chicken as . . .

Oscar Wilde: This chicken problem has many depths, but all of them are equally shallow.

Weekly World News: Nostradamus predicted chicken/UFO horror!

Charles Fort: Of course, I have heard of the "fourth dimension" but whatever is wrong with me has not advanced to the point where I will offer it as an explanation in a case like this. Maybe the damned chicken just wanted to see the other side. Maybe.

Hannibal Lecter: I ate her liver. With fava beans. And a fresh cranberry sauce.

the mgt

RAW would often sign his early emails, "the mgt." Over the years he changed his email signature many times. In private emails to friends he usually just signed, "bob," but in his emails to the Groupmind he became more creative. Some of his handles were, *Mark Chan, Mark the Wans, Mark the Tris, Damned Old Crank, Finnegan, Olga, RAW, Mark the Quark*, among others.

A lot of my emails with Bob were extensions of conversations we had during visits. A lot of our visits were us sharing stories of our various adventures. Advised by her friend Timothy Leary to leave Germany and travel West, vivacious and gregarious Marlis blazed a trail through the California New Age scene, and we had many stories to share with Bob about mystics, visionaries, health practitioners, artists, channelers, alternative scientists, shamans, gurus and a good number of what seemed to us to be charlatans. Bob loved it all, in part because he had his own stories with different versions of all of those same characters. Admittedly, in some ways, we were some of those characters ourselves.

When Tim Leary transcended the earthly plane, we were wondering if all of him actually did literally leave the earthly plane when his ashes were sent up into space. A movie came out that did a stellar job in making it look like Tim's head was removed and stored away until he could be safely unpacked in a more advanced future. I wrote to Bob about it and he replied, typically, with more delightful information than covered by the subject. Bob wrote,

> Yeah, I know Tim wanted to leave some Mystery behind. The film says his head was preserved.
>
> Everybody else says he was cremated and his ashes are circling the globe in a satellite.
>
> I got an email from him a month after his death saying the Other World wasn't what he expected -- "too crowded."
>
> Choose your reality-tunnel...
>
> bob
>
> Coinnigh an lasagne in airde!

Of all of us, I maintain that Bob was the better story teller. His often brief wry comments in emails to his friends sparkled like sugary brain candy. A lot of times he would simply send out a haiku, often inspired by whatever he saw in nature. Here are a few examples…

Grey and pastel pink --
A water-color painting --
This light before dawn.

All is cloaked in fog
The world seems empty, until --
Far off, a gull shrieks.

Mottled blueblack sky.
A sudden moon -- briefly! Then:
Blueblack mottled sky...

A number of times Marlis and I brought over a sitar and tamboura, and we gave mini-concerts in the Wilson living room. As lovers for many years, our non-traditional improvisations on the Indian instruments always felt to us a little like two lovers communicating through sound. I think Bob picked up on that. After one such visit, the next email from Bob contained an appreciation that always sounded to me like an extended haiku. Bob wrote,

"This music -- intricate yet melodic as Bach,
austere as a Zen shrine, sensory as a massage--
seems like aural eroticism to me"

Bob deeply appreciated all the dimensions of eroticism. Of the constellation of friends and family around Bob, his wife Arlen was his North Star. Often when Arlen was expounding on some subject, Bob would gaze at her as if a Philosopher Queen had just entered the room. Sometimes he would quote her in his email signature. This particular quote was actually Arlen's last words to Bob,

I am looking for a place
Where the horizon is all sky.
   Arlen Riley Wilson

Robert Anton Wilson was a curious mixture of brilliant intellect and inquisitive romantic. Most people who met Bob in person were pleasantly astounded by his humble and kind behavior. I'm hesitant to incorrectly recall things I heard him say in person, but fortunately, I still have all his old emails. Once, in a discussion about the therapeutic effects of ingesting calcium, a friend asked him about dealing with anxiety. Bob responded to the Groupmind,

> I had frequent bouts of anxiety in my early 20s and know how crippling it can feel. I tried Reichian therapy, Rational therapy, applying wot I knew of General Semantics, and some kind of "calcium." I don't know about the source or "morals" of the calcium.
>
> I also don't know which helped the most. Sometimes I think the "cure" came from loving and being loved by Arlen.
>
> TRY EVERYTHING that might help and don't let no fookin' puritans persuade you that you have a DUTY to suffer.
>
> & as usual, screw the Tsar!
>
> --bob

I don't want to paint a false picture of Robert Anton Wilson based on my love for my old friend. He could be ornery if pissed off, although he was usually still entertaining in his vexhood. When a publisher made an unwanted edit to a piece he submitted, he shared his response to the Groupmind,

> Dear Jason,
>
> "f***ing" shd read "fucking" or the whole point is lost, the sentence becomes oxymoronic, you censor and contradict what I assert, and my wailing ghost will haunt & vex you for all eternity.
>
> ARRRRRRRRRRRRRRGH!!!!!
>
> bob

Mostly, however, the guy was very sweet and generous, always giving credit to the efforts of others. He cc'd me once on an email he wrote to his son Graham. Graham had gotten the meme I made where Olga the ostrich was being interviewed on CNN.

Graham was wondering if there was some veracity involved. Graham wrote,

what's the story behind this attachment? was it from an actual story on CNN? or is it from computer enhanced graphics? (either way it's funny as hell and i love it but i am curious...is/was it from an actual story on CNN?)

Bob replied,

> A computer joke by my talented friend Rasa...
> When they let Olga [or me] on CNN pigs will fly
>
> love,
>
> dad

There are a lot of videos online, so it is easy to experience something from Robert Anton Wilson's soft soul. I heard him use the terms "cult" and "religion" interchangeably more than once, but he considered Buddhism to be in a different category for a number of reasons. In an August, 2001 email, after a visit where he had mentioned that he often chanted the Buddhist mantra, *Namu Amida Butsu*, I wrote,

> Marlis was sitting on the side of Mt. Shasta the other day with her eyes closed singing Namu Amida Butsu with a nice melody, and someone asked her what the tune meant. She knew the gist, but couldn't remember the Goddess.

Bob replied,

> I don't know the whole story but Amida is the Japanese name for a Hindic sage whose original name was something like Amittasa; he swore never to enter Nirvana until every sentient being entered along with him; somehow in China he got mixed up or merged with Kuan Yin, goddess of infinite mercy; I hear tell that you gotta be an Expert in Chinese art to tell if a given statue represents him or her.
>
> Namu Amida Butsu means "In the name of Amida Buddha." Orthodox Amida Buddhists say that if you utter those words once WITH TRUE FAITH you'll get to Nirvana eventually even if you're such a rotter it takes a few thousand incarnations.
>
> Shinran, a splinter off Amida Buddhism, sez true faith is not required; Amida won't reject you for having doubts.

Bob was big on "doubt." He thought the world would be far more sane if we all just used the word, "maybe" a whole lot more. In *Quantum Psychology* he lamented,

> "... one virtually never hears "*Maybe* Jesus was the son of God" or "*Maybe* Islam is a false religion.""

In *The New Inquisition*, Bob says,

> I am merely suggesting, playfully at times, maybe seriously at other times, that Universe is a bit more complicated than anybody's models; and that using several reality-tunnels – as in Po or quantum mechanics – *may* show a great many interesting correlations and details and exciting and beautiful aspects that we will never see if we look always and only through one monotonous reality-tunnel which we have made into an Idol.

One time Marlis gave Bob a book about conspiracies that was banned in Germany, *Secret Societies and Their Power in the 20th Century*, by one Jan van Helsing, an author who claimed to be an authority on the subject, and fearing retribution, chose a pseudonym borrowed from Stoker's famous vampire killer. We were fascinated by the book in the same way you might be fascinated by reading something about QAnon. Jan seemed to be a right-wing antisemitic conspiracy nut, but he covered so many subjects that RAW had written about, we were all a bit fascinated by the detailed insanity. I was fascinated by the many photos of Nazi Vril flying saucers included in the book. That was kinda cool, but overall, the book, published in 1995, so new for us at the time, seemed like a good representation of the kind of right wing nuttery Kerry, Greg and Bob lampooned when they promoted Operation Mindfuck and Discordianism.

Bob and I were both reading the book at the same time, and I wrote to him,

> I wonder about your take on the book Marlis gave you. Can these secret societies be simultaneously so successfully secret and also so slipshod that one CAN become an Authority on them?

Bob wrote back,

> That, sir, is the nub of the matter. As Israel Regardie once told me, "Paranoia is a disease of the ego." To believe in any of these cosmic conspiracy tomes one must believe that the conspirators are diabolically clever but the author is even more clever than they are.

In April of 2004, Bob had a short stay in the hospital after a fall, presumably brought on by his struggles with post-polio syndrome. We went to visit him, and afterwards I wrote an email to the Groupmind (Marlis made a few videos, and so the quotes below are accurate – verbatim taken from the videos). Here's most of what I wrote,

We asked Bob what happened to him. He said he was walking in his apartment and suddenly felt so weak he just let himself down to the floor, but then he didn't have the strength to get up again. He was on the floor for perhaps 30 hours before his daughter, Christina, knocked on the door. Even then, he called out and said, 'I'm here. I'm okay.' He talked about his thoughts during all those hours, but I'll let him relay that info, as I imagine it may make for interesting reading in the future.

The doctors are arguing over what's happening with him. Bob seems both amused and annoyed that they can't agree on what's going on with his health, and yet they always act like they know what's best for him. As for the diagnosis, Bob said laughing, "They all agreed that it was post-polio basically, he (one doctor) thought it might be something else basically. He changed his mind as he went through my bibliography, and went through all the scientific tests too, of course, and thought it was post-polio and either the weather, the flu, (laughs) somebody put a black magic spell on me . . ." Bob admitted the doctor didn't actually suggest the black magic, but he said, "Perhaps he will next week."

One doctor thought it was arthritis, another the effects of an imperceptible heart attack ten years in the past that has now complicated the post-polio syndrome. Bob said, "When you start thinking about real causality in the real world it looks much more complicated than it is in philosophical books and in theories." I asked Bob if they factored in the Republican Party. He said "They should."

Meanwhile Bob calls the head nurse "Big Nurse" in defiant homage. Bob says he's only allowed to answer Yes or No. They have no room for Maybe. He magnanimously pointed out that of all the hospitals to be in, he was in a very good one. Indeed the atmosphere was sunny and calm, but it is an institution. In opposition to conformist mentalities Bob insisted, "I am not like the 'average' post-polio patient."

Bob looks a little banged up from his struggle on the floor, some bruises on his face, arms and legs, but he's otherwise in good spirits - feisty, compassionate and humorous as always. To cheer him up, we took the stuffing out of a purple pooka, and inserted a bottle of Jameson Irish Whiskey, Bob's favorite libation. He loved that.

He had just gotten out of bed when I took the photo on the next page, so he had a wild case of hospital bed hair.

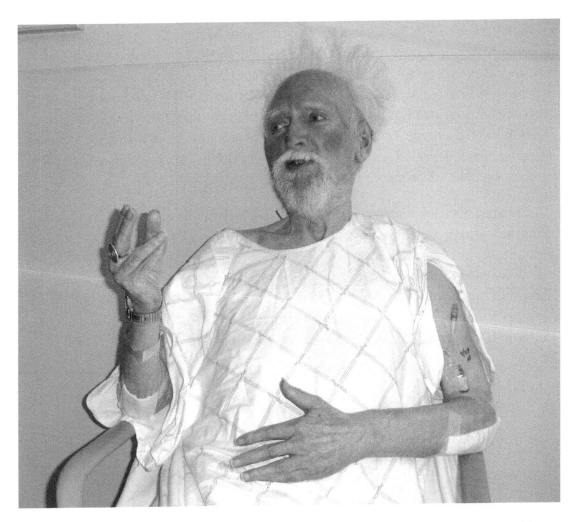

I told him he looked like he had just been plugged in. He felt his hair with his hand, and said, 'I guess I have something in common with Einstein after all.'

I asked Bob if he had any message for the Groupmind. He thought for a moment and then said, "Tell them I've learned a lot while in the hospital. I'm ready to write the sequel to Kafka's, *The Trial*."

I visited Bob one last time in 2007, about a week before he passed. He was so weak that his speech was a bit garbled, the result of muscle deterioration from the post-polio. At one point, he apologized to me because he thought I was struggling to understand what he was saying. That nearly brought me to tears. I told him that my head and heart were so full of his many words and ideas I absorbed over the years that no apology was necessary. Even as his body was failing him, his mind remained as sharp as ever, and what was on his mind was his consideration for others.

Bob loved his friend Tim Leary's acronym for a desirable future, SMI²LE: *Space Migration, Intelligence Increase, Life Extension*. In Bob's case, I would add C² to that formula: *Conscious Compassion*.

Christina once told me that when his post-polio symptoms began to hinder his habits, he started getting grumpy and sometimes a bit short-tempered with others, but then, one day he had a realization.

"Why would anyone want to help me if I'm being an ass?" Bob explained to Christina.

Christina says that after that, "He was radically different. He had had a multi-dimensional shift. He made a conscious decision to be different."

I couldn't sum up his life's work better than that, "He made a conscious decision to be different."

Rasa and Bob, 2004

Robert Anton Wilson Books
by Publication Date:

1 - Playboy's Book of Forbidden Words (1972)

2 - The Sex Magicians (1973)

3 - Sex and Drugs: A Journey Beyond Limits
    (1973 - Sex, Drugs and Magick: A Journey Beyond Limits 1988)

4 - The Book of the Breast (1974)

5 - The Eye in the Pyramid (The Illuminatus! Trilogy 1975) (with Robert Shea)

6 - The Golden Apple (The Illuminatus! Trilogy 1975) (with Robert Shea)

7 - Leviathan (The Illuminatus! Trilogy 1975) (with Robert Shea)

8 - Cosmic Trigger I: The Final Secret of the Illuminati (1977)

9 - Neuropolitics (1978) (with Timothy Leary and George Koopman)

10 - The Game of Life (1979) (with Timothy Leary)

11 - The Universe Next Door (Schrödinger's Cat Trilogy (1979)

12 - The Illuminati Papers (1980)

13 - The Trick Top Hat (Schrödinger's Cat Trilogy (1981)

14 - The Homing Pigeons (Schrödinger's Cat Trilogy (1981)

15 - Masks of the Illuminati (1981)

16 - The Earth Will Shake (The Historical Illuminatus Chronicles 1982)

17 - Prometheus Rising (1983)

18 - Right Where You Are Sitting Now (1983)

19 - The Widow's Son (The Historical Illuminatus Chronicles 1985)

HILARITAS
PRESS

Publishing the Books of Robert Anton Wilson
and Other Adventurous Thinkers
www.hilaritaspress.com

ffeith **IAU** PLANHIGION

Coed

@ebol

Coed

Cynnwys

Y fersiwn Saesneg
Cyhoeddwyd gan © Blake Publishing, 655 Parramatta Road, Leichhardt, NSW 2040, Awstralia.
Cedwir y cyfan o'r hawliau.
Ysgrifennwyd gan Paul McEvoy
Ymgynghorydd Gwyddoniaeth: Dr Will Edwards, Ysgol Bioleg Drofannol,
Prifysgol James Cook
Dylunio a gosod gan The Modern Art Production Group
Lluniau gan Photodisc, Stockbyte, John Foxx, Corbis, Imagin, Artville a Corel

Y fersiwn Cymraeg

Noddwyd gan Lywodraeth Cynulliad Cymru

ISBN 1-905255-62-4

Addasiad Cymraeg gan Glyn a Gill Saunders Jones
Dyluniwyd gan: stiwdio@ceri-talybont.com
Aelodau'r Pwyllgor Monitro:
Helen Lloyd Davies, Ysgol Penrhyn-coch, Aberystwyth
Gwenda Francis, Ysgol Melin Gruffydd, Caerdydd
Nia Jones, AADG
Argraffwyd gan: Gwasg Gomer, Llandysul

Beth ydy coeden?

Planhigyn gyda boncyff tal a changhennau ydy coeden. Mae angen aer, dŵr a golau haul ar goed i fyw a thyfu.

Mae gan goeden foncyff hir sydd wedi'i orchuddio â rhisgl. Mae'r boncyff yn cynnal y canghennau ac yn cadw'r goeden yn uchel uwchlaw'r ddaear. Mae'r rhisgl yn farw. Mae'r rhisgl yn amddiffyn y boncyff byw sydd y tu mewn. Mae'r boncyff yn tyfu'n fwy trwchus ac yn dalach bob blwyddyn.

Mae llawer o ganghennau yn tyfu ar goed. Mae'r canghennau yn ymestyn allan i bob cyfeiriad tua'r goleuni. Mae mwy a mwy o ganghennau yn tyfu bob blwyddyn.

Mae dail yn tyfu ar y canghennau. Mae canopi o ddail yn gorchuddio'r goeden. Mae'r dail yn defnyddio egni'r haul i gynhyrchu bwyd i'r goeden gyfan.

Mae gwreiddiau'r goeden yn tyfu o dan y ddaear. Mae gwreiddiau yn **amsugno** dŵr a maetholynnau o'r pridd. Mae angen dŵr ar goed i fyw a thyfu. Hefyd, mae'r gwreiddiau yn angori'r goeden i'r ddaear pan fydd y gwynt yn chwythu.

dail

canghennau

boncyff

gwreiddiau
o dan y
ddaear

Mae pob coeden gyda boncyff, canghennau, dail a
gwreiddiau. Mae pob rhan o'r goeden yn bwysig.

Cylch bywyd coeden

Mae coed yn fyw. Fel popeth byw mae coed yn tyfu, yn newid ac yn atgynhyrchu. Mae'r goeden fwyaf hyd yn oed wedi dechrau o'r hedyn lleiaf.

1 Mae coeden newydd yn dechrau tyfu pan fydd hedyn yn disgyn o'r gangen. Mae'r hedyn yn gallu disgyn i'r ddaear neu mae'n cael ei gario gan anifeiliaid, y gwynt neu ddŵr. Mae angen dŵr a gwres ar hedyn i ddechrau tyfu.

2 Mae gwreiddiau bach yn tyfu i mewn i'r ddaear i chwilio am ddŵr. Mae blaguryn gwyrdd yn tyfu tuag at oleuni'r haul. Bydd yn rhaid i'r goeden ifanc ddechrau cynhyrchu ei bwyd ei hunan.

3 Mae'r coed ifanc yn tyfu tuag at yr haul. Maen nhw'n tyfu'n syth ac yn dal.

4 Wrth i'r goeden aeddfedu mae'n blodeuo. Mae hadau newydd yn tyfu o'r blodau.

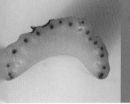

Sut mae coed yn yfed dŵr?

Mae coed yn yfed dŵr trwy eu gwreiddiau. Sut mae'r dŵr yn symud i ben eithaf y goeden?

Gwnewch yr arbrawf yma.

Bydd angen:

- seleri ffres
- jar wydr
- lliw bwyd (mae coch yn ddewis da)

Beth nesa?

1 Dewiswch goes seleri sydd gyda dail arni. Torrwch y rhan isaf.

2 Tywalltwch ychydig o'r lliw bwyd i mewn i'r jar wydr. Rhowch y seleri yn y lliw.

3 Rhowch y jar mewn lle heulog. Arhoswch am 15 munud.

4 Torrwch y seleri fesul darn i fyny'r coesyn. Pa mor bell y mae'r lliw wedi symud i fyny'r coesyn?

Mae'r lliw yn symud i fyny coes y seleri trwy diwbiau cul. Mae pob un o'r tiwbiau yma yn debyg i welltyn yfed!

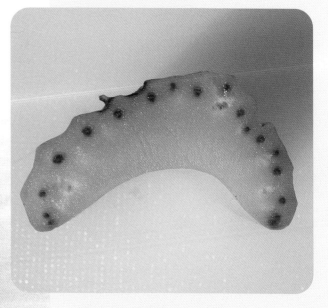

Mae'r lliw wedi cyrraedd y dail.

Mae coes y seleri yn sefyll mewn lliw bwyd.

9

Mathau o goed

Mae tri math o goed gwahanol. Y tri math ydy coed conwydd, coed palmwydd a choed llydanddail. Maen nhw i'w gweld mewn pob siâp a maint.

Coed Conwydd

Coed tal gyda boncyff syth a dail hir a chul neu nodwyddau ydy coed **conwydd**. Mae'r dail hirfain yn gallu dioddef gaeafau oer ac eira trwm. Mae'r rhan fwyaf o goed conwydd yn goed **bytholwyrdd**. Dydy'r coed yma ddim yn colli eu dail yn y gaeaf.

Mae coed conwydd yn cynhyrchu moch coed fel hadau. Coed conwydd ydy coed cedrwydd a choed pinwydd. Mae'r Coed Coch Mawr *(Giant Redwoods)* hefyd yn goed conwydd.

coedwig o goed conwydd

mochyn coed

palmwydd y gneuen goco

Coed Palmwydd

Boncyff syth sydd gan goed palmwydd. Does dim canghennau ar y boncyff. Mae dail coed palmwydd yn tyfu o ben y boncyff. Mae'r dail yn debyg iawn i siâp pluen neu fwa.

Mae coed palmwydd yn cynhyrchu hadau tu mewn i'r ffrwyth. Mae pobl yn bwyta rhai o ffrwythau'r coed palmwydd - ffrwythau fel cnau coco a datys.

palmwydd datys

11

Coed llydanddail

Y **rhywogaeth** mwyaf cyffredin ydy **coed llydanddail**. Mae'r dail ran amlaf yn wastad ac yn llydan.

Mae dail llydan a gwastad yn gallu casglu dŵr a goleuni'r haul. Mae rhai coed llydanddail yn goed **collddail** sy'n colli eu dail yn y gaeaf. Mae coed derw, coed masarn a choed poplys i gyd yn colli eu dail yn y gaeaf.

Mae gan rai coed fel y gelynnen a'r goeden oren ddail llydan bytholwyrdd. Mae'r goeden oren yn tyfu mewn ardaloedd cynhesach. Dydy'r coed yma ddim yn colli eu dail. Mae dail trwchus ac olewog gan y coed yma. Mae'r dail yn gallu bod yn fawr, yn fach, yn hir neu'n fyr.

Mae coed llydanddail yn blanhigion sy'n blodeuo. Mae hadau newydd yn tyfu o'r blodau. Mae rhai hadau yn cael eu cario gan y gwynt neu gan ddŵr. Mae anifeiliaid hefyd yn cario ffrwythau sy'n cynnwys hadau.

Mae'r dderwen yn goeden gollddail.

Mae'r goeden oren yn fytholwyrdd.

Mae dail coed masarn yn newid eu lliw yn yr hydref.

13

Coed a'r tymhorau

Mae'r rhan fwyaf o goed llydanddail yn colli eu dail yn y gaeaf. Maen nhw'n colli eu dail pan fydd golau dydd yn lleihau a'r tywydd yn troi'n oerach. Mae coed sy'n colli eu dail yn y gaeaf yn cael eu galw yn goed collddail.

1

Gwanwyn

Wrth i'r tywydd gynhesu mae'r blagur yn agor. Mae'r goeden yn deilio. Bydd rhai coed yn blodeuo.

14

Haf

2

Mae'r goeden yn tyfu.
Mae'r dail gwyrdd yn rhoi bwyd
i'r goeden gyfan.

Hydref

3

Fel mae'r tywydd yn
dechrau oeri a'r dydd yn byrhau,
mae'r bwyd yn symud o'r dail i'r
boncyff a'r gwreiddiau. Mae'r
dail yn colli eu lliw gwyrdd.
Mae'r dail yn troi'n sych ac yn
frau. Wedi i'r dail farw maen
nhw'n disgyn i'r llawr.

Gaeaf

4

Dydy coeden gollddail
ddim yn tyfu yn ystod y gaeaf.
Mae'r goeden yn dal yn fyw.
Mae'n rhaid aros am dywydd
cynnes cyn y bydd y goeden yn
tyfu unwaith eto.

Coedwigoedd

Mae llawer o goed yn tyfu mewn coedwig. Mae coedwigoedd yn gorchuddio mwy na chwarter arwynebedd y Ddaear. Mae llawer o fathau gwahanol o goedwigoedd i'w gweld. Maen nhw'n cynnwys coedwigoedd pinwydd a choedwigoedd glaw.

Ran amlaf, mae coed yn tyfu gyda'i gilydd i greu coedwig. Mae angen golau haul ar bob planhigyn. Mae coed uchel yn derbyn llawer o heulwen. Gan fod y dail yn uchel uwchlaw'r ddaear mae llai o anifeiliaid yn amharu ar y tyfiant.

coedwigoedd pinwydd

Mae coed yn tyfu mewn ardaloedd sy'n wahanol iawn i'w gilydd. Ran amlaf, ble mae'r glawiad yn uchel mae'r coed yn drwchus iawn.

Mae **coedwigoedd glaw** trofannol yn tyfu mewn ardaloedd gwlyb a phoeth yn ymyl y **Cyhydedd**. Mae pob math o goed llydanddail a bytholwyrdd yn tyfu yn y coedwigoedd yma. Coedwig law yr Amazon yn Brasil ydy'r goedwig law fwyaf yn y byd.

16

Coedwig law drofannol yn Brasil.

Mae coedwigoedd glaw hefyd i'w gweld mewn ardaloedd tymherus.

17

Coed yn addasu i'w hamgylchedd

Mae coedwigoedd conwydd yn tyfu mewn ardaloedd sy'n ffinio â Phegwn y Gogledd. Yn yr ardaloedd yma, mae eira yn gorchuddio'r coedwigoedd am sawl mis yn y gaeaf. Mae'r coed gyda'u nodwyddau caled yn gwrthsefyll y tywydd oer yn ystod y gaeaf.

Mae coedwigoedd tymherus yn tyfu ble mae'r tywydd yn gynhesach. Mae'r ardaloedd yma yn cael rhwng pedwar a chwe mis o dywydd cynnes mewn blwyddyn. Mae nifer o wahanol fathau o goed yn tyfu yma. Un math diddorol o goeden ydy'r Goeden Goch Fawr *(Giant Redwood)* sy'n tyfu yng nghoedwigoedd California. Mewn coedwigoedd collddail tymherus mae'r dderwen a'r fasarnen yn tyfu. Yn Awstralia, mae'r goeden ewcalyptws yn goeden gyffredin iawn.

ewcalyptws

coedwig o goed pinwydd

coedwig o goed
coch mawr

ffeithIAU!

YR HYNAF!

Wyddoch chi mai'r Wollemi,
pinwydden yn Awstralia, ydy un
o goed hynaf y byd? Roedd y
goeden yma i'w gweld pan
oedd deinosoriaid yn cerdded y
ddaear!

19

Coed fel cartrefi

Mae llawer o anifeiliaid yn byw mewn coed. Mae coed yn rhoi bwyd a chysgod i'r mwnci a'r wiwer - heb sôn am adar a thrychfilod amrywiol.

Mae'r rhan fwyaf o fwncïod yn byw ac yn bwyta mewn coedwigoedd. Maen nhw hefyd yn dianc i'r coed rhag anifeiliaid sy'n eu hela ar lawr y goedwig. Mae mwncïod wedi addasu i'w bywyd yn y coed. Mae eu cynffonnau yn eu helpu i neidio o gangen i gangen.

Mae nifer o famaliaid bach yn byw yn y coed. Mae coed yn rhoi cysgod rhag y gwynt, y glaw ac anifeiliaid eraill. Mae ambell dwll mewn boncyff yn rhoi cartref cysurus i'r wiwer. Mae'r mes hefyd yn cynnig pryd blasus i'r wiwer. Mae'r coala yn byw a bwyta mewn coed ewcalyptws.

Coala

Mae llawer iawn o adar yn byw yn y coed. Maen nhw'n adeiladu eu nythod ar gangen neu mewn cilfach gyfleus. Mae coed yn rhoi bwyd fel ffrwythau, neithdar a hadau i'r adar.

Mae miliynau o drychfilod yn byw mewn un goeden. Mae pob math o chwilod, morgrug a gloÿnnod byw yn dibynnu ar goed fel lle i gysgodi a chael pryd o fwyd!

20

Os bydd cyfle mae'r racŵn yn gwneud ei gartref mewn boncyff gwag.

Mae'r gorila hefyd yn teimlo'n gartrefol yn byw yn y coed.

Mae rhai adar yn nythu yn y coed.

Coed, blodau a hadau

Math o goeden	Ydy hi'n blodeuo?	Ydy hi'n fytholwyrdd?	Ble mae'r hadau?
palmwydden cneuen goco	ydy	ydy	cneuen goco
derwen	ydy	nac ydy	mesen
pinwydden	nac ydy	ydy	mochyn coed
lemon	ydy	ydy	lemon
bricyllen	ydy	nac ydy	bricyllen
celynnen	ydy	ydy	aeron

Geirfa

amsugno	llyncu, sugno
bytholwyrdd	coed sydd ddim yn colli eu dail i gyd dros y gaeaf. Coed sy'n deilio'n wyrdd drwy'r flwyddyn
coed conwydd	enw arall arnyn nhw ydy coed coniffer. Maen nhw'n cynnwys pinwydd, ffynidwydd a'r cedrwydd. Coed sydd gan amlaf yn fytholwyrdd. Yr hadau ydy moch coed.
coed llydanddail	coed dail llydan fel y dderwen a'r onnen sydd fel arfer yn colli eu dail yn yr hydref - er bod rhai coed llydanddail fel y gelynnen ddim yn colli eu dail
coed collddail	coed sy'n colli eu dail yn y gaeaf
coedwig law	coedwig drwchus sy'n tyfu mewn ardal boeth sy'n derbyn glaw trwm
cyhydedd	llinell ar fap sydd hanner ffordd rhwng Pegwn y Gogledd a Phegwn y De sy'n rhannu'r byd yn ddwy ran gyfartal
rhywogaeth	teulu neu ddosbarth o blanhigion neu anifeiliaid o'r un fath
trofannol	gair sy'n disgrifio rhywbeth sy'n perthyn i'r Trofannau neu sy'n nodweddiadol o'r Trofannau (yn arbennig y tywydd poeth)

23

Mynegai